Miracles of
Childlike Faith

BASED ON A TRUE STORY
that will forever touch your heart

AMMIE L. PETERS

Published by:
Blessings 2 Good, Inc.

Miracles of Childlike Faith
Copyright © 2012 by Blessings 2 Good, Inc.

International Standard Book Number: 978-0-9847722-5-4
Library of Congress Number: 2012954824
Revision 1.3 09/26/17

Cover design by: Susan Doctor
Cover photo by: Joe Prible

Acknowledgments

Thank you God for never giving up on me, loving me unconditionally, teaching me how to love others unconditionally and for the precious gift of childlike faith.

"And Yahushua looking upon them said to them. With men this is impossible; but with Yahweh all things are possible."

Matthew 19:26

My life is a living testimony of that beautiful Truth.

Note from Author

"Miracles of Childlike Faith" is a true story about my Life. Although I publish under the name Ammie, the birth name given to me by my mother (Pam) and father (Ted) is Sandra so you will see references to "Sandi" throughout the pages. When I share with others that I write under a different name sometimes I get a puzzled look, some even ask the question bluntly "is it so no one knows who you are?" I smile and answer "no, not at all". Being given the name Ammie is one of my most cherished gifts.

I'll never forget the moment I knew I was to write under that name. After praying about it, I saw a Hand appear before me that wrote "Ammie" in big letters. I asked, "How do you say it?" I had never heard of or even seen this name before. The response was, "*It doesn't matter how you say it, it's who you are.*" I'll just take a moment to say, "Yes, I hear God." :) It is one of the many things I have been blessed with since the time of the miracles. I hear God's Voice within my Heart, within my Spirit, as clearly as I hear someone speaking to me. When I heard *Ammie is who I am*, I had chills run through me. I knew this name being given to me was very important. I wasn't shown the last name at the same time but a few days later, while on the treadmill, the name "Peters" was spoken to me. I said, "Peters. Really? Peters?" not that there is anything wrong with that name but I was surprised at its simplicity and how common it is. It then pressed on my Heart to look up the meaning of this new name I had been given. I saw Ammie L. Peters (the L. being my middle name of Lynn that my parents gave me at birth). I looked up each name and was in awe. Ammie (I pronounce as AM-ME) means "Beloved". Lynn means "Waterfall" and Peters means "Rock" ... Beloved Waterfall Rock. I had tears in my eyes as my Heart overflowed with thankfulness for this new name.

Imagine my surprise a couple of years later when I found out from my brother that he had researched our family genealogy and our maternal great grandmother's maiden name was Peters. Seriously?!? Yes, seriously! God never ceases to amaze me. My brother then began to share how we are Jewish on both the father and mother bloodlines, even royalty from our father's side. God is full of wonderful surprises and I can only imagine what blessings will be next.

~~~~~~~~~~~~

After the miracles in my life, many things began to manifest. The dreams and visions written about in scripture were given to me at a rate that only God could give. I have chills as I write it. I have had dreams from the time I was a little girl but something even more powerful happened after I was touched by God's Hand ... The Hand that manifested miracle after miracle in my life. My experience has forever changed me, in ways I truly never thought were possible. I look forward to sharing my true story with you across these pages.

Years ago I wrote the first version of my story under "Blessings Too Good". It was without a doubt divinely inspired. I was so excited and wanted to get it out there right away. I just wanted to help people so much. It is what has been at the core of my being since the time I was a little girl. In my excitement, I failed to stop and ask God's input on *when* I was to share my story and *how*. Yeah, a wee bit of a caveat I must say and a hard lesson learned but I'm thankful for that lesson. With the best intentions, I had just wanted to get my story out there and right away. Did I say **right away**? :) Well, that's what I did. After saying that, I think it's an obvious precursor that one of the things I had to learn was patience and another was trusting God's timing. At the time, I didn't quite understand why I was facing roadblock after roadblock when trying to get it into the hands of people. It wasn't because the world was trying to stop me but rather God telling me "slow down little missy". He had to teach me much and ensure I understood the importance of sharing my story through the eyes and the Heart He specifically has given me. It wasn't to be shared thru the eyes of how the world saw Him (or taught) but through the eyes of simple childlike faith that I have.

So it is with great honor and such deep gratitude that I write this book in the simple language of childlike faith. For thru the eyes of a child, your Daddy is your Hero, your Protector, your Provider, your Life … you know no other option. He is all you know, all you need and the One you cling to even before you realize others call Him by a name different than "Daddy". You believe and that is exactly what I needed for the impossible to become possible in my life.

Table of Contents

Preface

"Our journey here begins with one step and only we can decide whether or not to take that step."

- *Ammie L. Peters*

I've learned a lot on my journey and continue to learn more each day. I've learned that Faith is a condition of the Heart and not something you do every Sunday. I've learned that Faith dwells within the Heart and no one knows the Heart except God. I've learned that Faith truly does move mountains. My story is one of trials and tribulations that most cannot imagine enduring but one that serves as a true testimony of the Living God and the miracles possible when we Believe.

From the time I was a little girl, I have seen things opposite of how the world sees things. I find the good in all things when the world sees the bad. I see hope when the world sees discouragement. I see possible when the world sees the impossible.

My story is simple but true.

As you take my hand and walk with me across the pages of this book, may you feel and experience the beautiful gift of childlike faith along with me. May this walk together through the ups and downs bring Life to the childlike faith in your very own Heart.

CHAPTER 1

When the Miracles Started
(Age 0)

"In this manner says Yahweh, your Redeemer, and he that formed you from the womb: I am Yahweh, that makes all things; that stretches forth the heavens along; that spread abroad the earth (who is with me?)" Isaiah 44:24

12/24/98 - I find myself once again in the hospital at the holidays. This time is much worse than the others. There's an urgency within my heart that is deeper than anything I have felt before. I yearn to be home with my son. He's four and I miss him so much. While the rest of the world is getting stressed with everything they have to do for Christmas, that stress would be a welcomed gift over what I'm facing right now. I sit here crying out to God praying for just one more day and being thankful for each breath He is giving me.

1

Something doesn't feel right, I can't breathe and I'm in so much pain throughout my abdomen that I can hardly stand it. But I keep holding onto the hope that somehow a miracle will get me home tonight. Deep inside I know without a miracle this will be my last Christmas with my family. I need to be home, please God, please get me home! The nurses know the chances are slim to none but I will not give up hope, there's always hope, always! It seems I am that person people refer to when they say, "if it is going to happen to anyone it's going to happen to her." Just this once, I would like to be normal instead of falling into that less than 1% of the population statistic. I mean who ends up in the hospital almost every holiday? Hope, there's always hope.

At the time of that journal entry, I didn't know what God had planned for my life nor did I know if He would send me a miracle and get me home for Christmas. But what I did know is that no matter what I had to hold on and never give up hope. I didn't know the plan but He did so I had to trust it. He then brought me back to the very beginning, age 0, to ensure I understood that the journey He planned for my life

2

started before I was born. I know it sounds cliché but the reality that there is a plan for each of our lives even before we are conceived didn't quite sink in until the moment I sat down to listen to my mom share the story of her pregnancy with me.

"Before I formed you in the belly I knew you, and before you came forth out of the womb I sanctified you; I have appointed you a prophet to the nations." Jeremiah 1:5

I never thought to ask her details other than the typical how much I weighed, how tall I was or how she felt during the pregnancy. I sat in awe of God when I listened to every word and was overcome with how not only His timing is perfect but how He knows us long before we are a twinkle in our daddy's eye. All these years and I knew parts of the story but couldn't have imagined what she was about to share.

"Well, honey it all started when your Dad and I knew it was time to start a family. It shouldn't have been a problem really because my side of the family let's just say there was a standing joke that just by your great grandpa hanging his pants on the bedpost grandma would get pregnant." She laughed as she said it. She continued, "We kept going to the doctor to get things checked out because no matter what we tried, we were not getting pregnant. Back then there weren't a lot of options like there are now and we even went to a specialist. Well, the specialist felt we were to try a procedure that would blow air into my fallopian tubes. It sounded kind of strange but I knew in my heart that we should try it." She paused for a minute looking up gently pressing her lips together, "I'm pretty sure it was on a Friday. Yes, it was a Friday because I remember the doctor telling us to go home and try to get pregnant right away and can you believe I got pregnant that very weekend?" I said, "Mom that's really cool, I had no idea! It says so much to me. It reminds me of God's breath and how He has to breathe life into us just like how the air had to be blown into your fallopian tube before a new little life could come into the world." I had chills as I said it. "I remember you saying something about a procedure with air but I didn't know all the other stuff."

"Oh there is more honey," she said.

"What? What do you mean more?" I said.

"Well from the moment I conceived I knew I was pregnant," she shared. "I waited until I was late and then went to the doctor for a checkup. He did a urine pregnancy test and said, "I'm sorry Pam but you are not pregnant." I said, "Doctor but I am pregnant." He then said, "Well let's do a blood test to be sure then." She continued, "They drew my blood and sent it off to the lab. The blood test showed negative too." The doctor told me I was not pregnant and that those two tests combined are 99.9% accurate. I told him, "I am pregnant. The tests are wrong." He looked at me like I was crazy but I knew I was pregnant. They waited a couple more weeks and tested me again with the urine and blood tests – both negative. But, I knew I was pregnant. I was even having morning sickness by then. Well right before the end of the first trimester I went to the doctor and insisted I was pregnant. He said he would do an internal exam to check everything out and ensure something else wasn't going on. I got on the examining table, put my feet in the stir-ups and the doctor began the exam. He looked completely flabbergasted and belted out, 'Oh my God, you are pregnant!' Well, of course I was! I knew it all along."

I sat there with my jaw open at what I just heard from my mom. "Mom, are you serious?" I asked in shock. She said, "Oh yes, honey. I am serious. Ask your dad how many times we had to go to the doctor." I sat there my mind drifting off for a minute thinking about how my whole life, starting from conception, fell into that 1% or less category of the population. Most often in my life it was amidst storms, the times when having the odds on your side would be a good thing. I quickly learned and became living proof that even odds of 1 in a million mean nothing when you have faith. Faith can truly move mountains. Wow, I mean this is ... I had no idea it started from conception. I got chills thinking of it. She had mentioned before they told her she wasn't pregnant when she was but that was the extent of it.

She went on, "And I kept having the same dream over and over during my pregnancy with you. I will never forget any of this, I will remember it forever."

"Don't leave me hanging like this, Mom. What was your dream?"

She said, "I kept dreaming I was going to have a little girl and that she had a full head of black hair longer than most babies' hair. What's funny is every time I had the dream, you would crawl out of my belly and you were so small that I could fit you in a shoebox and that is where I laid you all snuggled up and cozy." She giggled as if the whole dream was playing out in her mind. She continued, "I knew my little baby girl was going to be special and she is."

"Mom, why do you always say that? Everyone is special." She just smiled at me because we have had this same conversation hundreds of times.

5

"And boy your dad wondered what was going on with me."

"Why?"

"Well, when I was seven months pregnant I had all of the birth announcements filled out with everything but your height and weight. I knew you were a girl. I even knew exactly what your name was to be. I shared the name with your dad and he immediately agreed. I think it was the first thing in our lives that we had agreed on," she said as she laughed. "But he didn't necessarily agree I should be writing out the announcements, I mean you weren't going to be born for a few more months. I just knew it to be true with every part of my being. You were a girl and your name was to be Sandra Lynn no one could take that away from me."

"Really?"

"Yes. I knew my little girl was," I chimed in rolling my eyes as a half smiled crossed my face and I finished the sentence for her, "going to be special." We both just laughed.

"Well, I wasn't the only one who thought so," she said.

"What do you mean?"

"The nurses at the hospital completely spoiled you. The nursery was filled with babies but for some reason they all took turns holding you. I don't think I ever saw you in the crib. They held you all the time and even got you use to a pacifier by taking a baby bottle and filling the nipple with cotton even though it wasn't time for you to eat because they never wanted to hear you cry."

A soft smile spread across her lips and her eyes stared off for a second as if she was living the moment right then for the very first time. Her heart overflowed with so much Love that it filled the room and brought me into that moment with her. There we stood as if it was June 1968 standing outside of the baby nursery peeking thru the window together feeling the Love that filled every part of that nursery.

~~~~~~~~~~

Well that is where my journey begins. A baby girl born into a small town in Indiana whose life from conception has been a testimony of how all things are possible with God. A life that was destined to cling to hope despite being up against insurmountable odds, a life that would be filled with challenges and suffering that most cannot imagine enduring but all to serve as a testimony of what is possible when we believe.

CHAPTER 2

Daddy's Little Angel
(Age 6)

"You are the light of the world. A city set on a hill cannot be hid. Neither do men light a lamp, and put it under the bushel, but on the stand; and it shines to all that are in the house. Even so let your light shine before men, that they may see your good works and glorify your Father who is in heaven." Matthew 5:14-16

I was still in awe at what mom shared with me about her pregnancy with me so I called Dad to talk with him about it. He said he had something he wanted to share that he had never really told anyone. It's amazing to me how often we don't find out things until the exact time we need them. God's timing is always perfect and this was just another reminder of that timing. My dad began to share a treasure he has had in his heart for many years.

"Remember when you were about 6 or 7 years old and had to have bi-lateral hernia surgery?"

"Oh yes, I remember. I walked like an old lady for a week. And I still remember the special nightgown you and mom bought me. It was white with red and blue bows. Oh! And it had red and blue dots all over it too with a little ruffle around the bottom. They were my favorite pajamas. I felt so special."

"Well your dear old dad doesn't like to admit this but I was scared. I didn't want you having surgery and I was more than a worry wart about it – petrified to

8

tell you the truth. I was sitting in the waiting room while you and your mom walked down the hallway of the hospital. My hands were sweating worrying about what could happen to my little girl. About that time I looked up and saw you and your mom walking towards me. You had your gown on and your new little slippers, you looked so cute. Then I had to do a double-take to ensure my eyes weren't playing tricks on me. I saw this white Light all around you. You know how it looks when you see a picture of an Angel where it is kind of a soft, blended light surrounding them? Well as soon as I saw it, an instant peace came over me. I've never had anything like it before or after that time. At that minute, I knew you were going to be okay and that you were going to be doing something very special in this world."

"Dad why haven't you ever told me this before?"

"I didn't think anyone would understand it but now I know you will after all you've been through."

"That is so awesome! God is amazing. He's everywhere, Dad, everywhere and I want the world to know He is real and all that can happen when you believe. If people could just open their hearts and minds knowing He is in everything, their lives will be so blessed and filled with moments of peace like you received that day."

"I know honey, if everyone had the perspective God gave you what a wonderful world it would be."

"What do you mean Dad?"

"Well kiddo, you have always seen things differently – actually opposite of what most people see.

9

You find the good in everything and love everybody. But it wasn't easy growing up watching my little girl continue to put her heart out there and watch people walk all over it. No matter what I would tell you, you would keep going back and give them another chance. It's who you are. You never gave up on anyone because you always saw the good when no one else could find even one small good thing in that person. And it wasn't just in people, it was in everything."

"Like what?"

"Well let me say it this way. Imagine a house in black and white that has broken windows, busted shudders and weeds growing up all over the place. Everyone else would see a house that was an eyesore to the neighborhood and talk about how it's bringing the value of the neighborhood down. You would say, 'But daddy look at that flower.' And there amongst all the weeds was one beautiful flower rising up in color and that is all you saw. You looked past all of the other stuff and saw only the good. You taught your old man a thing or two that's for sure."

I had tears fill my eyes. Growing up at times I felt something was wrong with me because I always saw things so differently than others. I love the unloved and people judged me for it. I would say white, they would say black. I wondered why I was different and what was wrong with me but no matter how many tears I cried asking to be like others God would not change me. I felt I was on the island of the Land of the Misfit Toys and I was the first toy to arrive.

When dad shared this with me, I realized what a gift God had given me and how thankful I am that He didn't answer that prayer no matter how much I cried out asking Him to. It is what got me thru life and what would get me thru all that was coming up ahead. I focused on the good and had faith that all would work out no matter what the plan. I saw the flower in every situation and I want to help everyone else to see that flower instead of the brokenness around them.

He said, "Sam, you were always my little Angel with a heart the size of Texas. And no matter how much I would tell you that you couldn't help everyone because I didn't want you to get hurt and continue to be disappointed, you would not give up on anyone especially when the rest of the world did." He smiled a very approving smile proud that his little girl was determined to share her special heart with the world.

CHAPTER 3

Introduction of the Heart Tug
(Age 7)

"Whoever shall confess that Yahushua is the son of Yahweh, Elohim lives in him, and he in Elohim." **1 John 4:15**

It was summer time and mom had my sister, Susan, and I dressed in our new dresses and shoes all ready for Sunday school. I remember the first ride on the powder blue bus to a church an hour away in Hammond, IN. The children around me were singing songs that I didn't yet know so I felt a little uncomfortable. The songs quickly started to grow on me. The kids filed off the bus and formed a single line to go into our classroom. I'll never forget as we walked into the class, there was a table with cookies and Dixie cups half filled with red Kool-Aid. Each kid quickly learned that once the teachers were done talking about God that they would get this yummy treat which greeted them at the door every Sunday.

After class we would get paired up to walk over to the church. There a man with dark hair, dark eyes and a very gentle spirit stood at the front of the church teaching about God. He said that God's son, Jesus (aka Yahushua the original Hebrew name before translation to the name Jesus in English), came to teach us and show us how to live and to follow in his footsteps. The nice man said because of the sacrifice of Yahushua, God lives in our Hearts. He said that anyone who wanted to accept Yahushua could come up to the altar but I was too afraid. My parents weren't with me. I didn't know anyone so I stood at my seat with tears in my eyes from the truth of his message. I repeated the prayer to accept Yahushua into my Heart. His words then ran thru my thoughts again that now God lives in my heart. I looked down at my dress and thought, *"God that's a strange place for You to live and how in the world do You fit in there anyway?"* I knew if God lived in there then I better start paying more attention to my Heart.

That is the moment God taught me the Heart Tug. It was received into the Pure Heart of a little child. I knew it in my heart to be true. God being with us every minute and there to guide us to everything we need. I still hadn't figured out how He fit in there but I knew He was there. I believed.

As I got older, I would feel the Heart Tug to call someone out of nowhere to find it was the exact time they needed someone to be there for them. I would feel in my Heart to pick up extra food only to discover that we would have another mouth to feed at the dinner table that night. If I made a mistake and hurt someone's feelings, my Heart would let me know and keep reminding me until I set things right.

As I grew up, I learned the hard way that I need to always listen to the Heart Tug because the times I didn't is when things didn't go so great. I would enter into things my way and wonder later why things didn't go so great. But when I did listen, my Heart was at Peace and my ways were blessed. And those things in my Life where I did listen were not torn down because God built them one brick at a time. The things I built doing things my way He would tear down and that was never easy.

It wasn't until years later that I discovered others didn't know about the Heart Tug. I was surprised because I thought everyone knew about it just like everyone knows we need air to breath. I thought, *"How are people getting thru life if they are not listening to that Heart Tug?"*

CHAPTER 4

Childhood Memories
(Age 11)

"Beloved, let us love one another: for love is of Yahweh; and everyone that loves is begotten of Yahweh, and knows Yahweh."
1 John 4:7

Our family moved into a new subdivision when I was 5 years old. My baby sister, Susan, was 4 and my mom was pregnant with our baby brother Mike at the time. There were a lot of kids so we made many new friends. My mom stayed at home with us while my dad worked as a mechanic at Hardings, Inc. in Lowell, IN. He worked on the huge caterpillar tractors that were as big as giants. I'll never forget his blue uniform with the sewn on badge that read "Ted". He would come home smelling like a mix of motor oil and grease. Stains filled the crevices of his calloused hard-working hands. It's funny how the smell of oil and grease today instantly takes me back to my childhood and how much I love that smell because it reminds me of my dad. We were so proud of our dad who was smart enough to work on those huge tractors. He left every morning no later than 5:30 am and would always be home for dinner at 5 o'clock. He worked so hard and never missed a day no matter how sick he was.

Once Mikey was born and was old enough to play with us, we would all play in the backyard which consisted of mostly sand and sandburs (also known as stickers). Oh how we did not like those things! We would go out to play and come in with sandburs all over our shoelaces and if we fell while playing in the yard, boy did it hurt but it was a normal part of life to us. Dad would do everything to get rid of the sandburs but it took him years until the last one had finally become extinct in our yard! Mikey would sit in the sand for hours playing with his dump trucks while Susan and I would play on the swings.

Mom would call us in for dinner and we would always race to see who made it to the door first. Bending over, out of breath we would take off our shoes trying not to get poked with a sticker while untying our shoelaces– ouch! Those awful things we disliked so much would end up being the very thing to inspire the invention of Velcro, who knew? See there is good in everything – if we look for it we can find it, even in the smell of motor oil and the pain of a sticker that doesn't want to let go of your shoelace!

We didn't have a care in the world, we enjoyed being kids. We could safely ride our bikes up and down the streets. We left our doors unlocked and there were no worries of us playing outside until dark. It was safe. Life was simple. We looked forward to Dad coming home every day. Well, except the days we would get into trouble and were sent to our room being told, "You can stay in here and think about what you did until your Dad comes home." Those were some long days let me tell you. Most days we would be running up to Dad's car running alongside of him until he pulled into the driveway. We would greet him with the biggest hug we could. Mom and Dad love us so much. We didn't have a lot of extras but we always had unconditional love from both of them. Any time we would get spankings (yes in those days the rod was not spared), Dad would always say, "This hurts me more than it hurts you." I never understood that until I was older and had children of my own. We were reminded during those times of punishment that we were loved. It is important we understand that *we* weren't bad but our decision was and there are consequences to bad decisions. Dad told us things once and that was it or else there was trouble but no matter what we always knew our mom and dad loved us.

After dinner we would usually sit as a family and watch TV. We loved when Disney would have a special program. We would wait weeks for it to come on because cable TV did not exist so we didn't have the Disney channel available to watch at any time. We would watch our favorite shows becoming absorbed oblivious to all that surrounded us. It felt like no time had passed at all and then Dad would begin singing, "Good night ladies, good night ladies, good night laaaaadies it's time to go to bed." My sister and I would always look at each other with a big sigh, rolling our eyes because we knew it meant bed time and there was no negotiating.

We'd trot off to bed and get snuggled up under the homemade blankets mom had crocheted for our beds. Mine was dark pink with some light pink and Susan's was light pink with a little dark pink. We had twin beds side by side separated by a dresser in the middle. Each night we would lie in bed and talk before we drifted off to sleep. We were always getting yelled at for talking but realize now it's why they made us go to bed so early. Mom and Dad knew we would talk so despite hearing, "Girls quit talking or I'm coming up there." They allowed us our time for sisterly bonding. Sometimes we would push it a little too far and would keep talking despite the warning. We'll never forget the time we both heard Dad yell, "Girls do you want to get up?" We looked at each other not believing they were letting us get up and said, "Yes!" as we jumped out of bed. We ran downstairs and he said, "You put your nose in that corner and you put your nose in that corner until you understand what it means to be quiet and go to sleep". It only took once of falling asleep standing in a corner to learn after the first warning it's time to get quiet and go to sleep.

Our days were filled with playing. We kept Mom busy most of the time. Dad would work and then tinker in the garage a lot with the cars. Well one Saturday morning when I was 11 years old, mom and dad called us into the house and sat us down. My heart dropped, I knew instantly something was wrong but I had no idea what they were about to share with us. They told us that we have to understand they love us very much and nothing we did made this happen but they were getting a divorce. I felt like I was just hit by a truck because I don't remember Mom and Dad ever arguing so it came as a shock, a big surprise. I respect my parents trying to do the right thing not arguing in front of us but honestly I would have rather had them be real in front of us. It's not easy for people to do that in the world but it's important. We did not see this coming at all. It began a shift in our lives that would forever change us. Mom found herself in a situation where she had to get a job with no work experience because she had always stayed at home to take care of us. Dad found himself in a position where he had no extra money, not even enough to eat half the time after paying child support and rent. I'll never forget how much weight he lost and how each time we visited Dad we would eat fried bologna because it's all he could afford. Mom struggled with working, taking care of us and trying to balance everything. We would see Dad on most weekends but not during the week which was hard at first but then we adjusted.

During the time of the divorce, I went from being a happy kid who did well in school to a kid who couldn't focus on her grades and soon found her "A" in Social Studies dropping all the way down to a "D". I tried to focus on the good as well as a child could so soon found my thoughts focusing on the good news of how I had made the 5th grade cheerleading team. I had practiced so hard putting my whole heart into learning the cheers and gymnastic moves. I couldn't believe that I had made it!!! It was such a gift in the middle of this hard time of my life. Well, as I type this today tears well in my eyes as I drift back to the memory of sitting in my 5th grade classroom and finding out thru an announcement over the intercom that I was being replaced on the cheerleading team. A big congratulations to the new cheerleader belted out thru the speaker system and echoed thru the halls. It's as if it penetrated every cell of my being. As the class applauded, I sat quietly crying at my desk so embarrassed. I sat there feeling all alone in a world that I didn't seem to fit in. I thought, "Why do I always have to be so different? Why do things always happen to me?" I began to cry even more.

When I got home from school my mom asked me what was wrong after seeing the red swollen eyes overpowering her daughter's face. She just held me as I cried and tried to get the words out in between the sobs. She was so upset that the school handled things the way that they did without talking to my parents first. She held me, told me she was sorry and I could see her heart breaking along with mine. It was a valuable lesson teaching me the importance of empathy – the ability to truly put ourselves in another's shoes. When we use the eyes of our Heart instead of the eyes in our head to look at a situation, we notice things like a little girl not being herself with dropping grades and caring enough to love her instead of frowning upon her "lack of effort" and so easily ripping away a dream that happened to be the bare thread she was holding onto at that time of her life.

After a while, Mom then started dating and later got married so our family grew to include our step dad, Ron who I nicknamed king and he nicknamed me princess. He lived in Arkansas so Mom ended up moving there. She would call all the time and we would spend the summers with her but we missed her a lot and she cried a lot when she called. I remember it seemed the rest of the world didn't understand her moving away but in my heart somehow I did even at that young age. I knew she was going to play a very important role in Ron's life but was too young to articulate what my Heart was feeling. My dad also remarried and his new wife had 3 children of her own. We were soon just like the Brady Bunch minus the maid of course. We had to learn to go without and share everything including a room, clothes, etc. Two families coming together was not easy but we made it. I mean how many people could say they were like the Brady Bunch, right?

We settled into a routine, got use to spending our summers with Mom and Ron in the smoldering heat of Arkansas but loved coming home every summer with a dark tan as a result of spending time outside in a place that seemed so different it almost felt like another world. I mean the dirt there is red not brown or black like the soil in Indiana. There were also caves and rivers and cliffs to jump off of so although it was hard being away from Dad in the summer, we had some nice memories in good old Arkansas.

Seemed the school year would fly by and soon it would be time to head down to another hot summer in Arkansas with Mom and Ron. I enjoyed school because I was surrounded by people and enjoyed seeing how differently we are made. And how love at the Heart can connect us all no matter what worlds we come from, love has a way of breaking down walls. I would want to cheer someone up or encourage them because from deep in my Heart I have always wanted everyone to be happy, to be who God made them to be and to be at peace with who they are. I didn't expect anything in return but the gift of seeing a smile on a once dreary face because of something you say or do really makes the Heart feel great.

You know thinking back to my junior high days at Mt. Ayr Junior High in Mt. Ayr, Indiana there was something that really impacted me during that time of my life. I was in 8th grade when the World's Fair was coming to the United States. It was going to be in Knoxville, TN and there was a field trip offered for kids from our school to go as a group and be able to experience it. I really wanted to go knowing the opportunity it would be but we couldn't afford it so I didn't have the heart to even ask my dad. He worked so hard and I didn't want him to feel bad that we didn't have the money. I sat watching the kids with excitement knowing it was coming up soon and so desperately wanting to be part of it. But I had learned to be content with little and to be thankful for what we did have although it wasn't much compared to others.

I walked into class and sat down quietly as the other kids beamed with excitement about the upcoming trip. Although I was sad that I couldn't go, I was really happy for them. About that time my teacher came up and wanted to talk with me. She told me that they had given her a ticket for one of the children to go for free and wanted to know if I would like to go. I looked up at her and said, "Really?" with tears filling my eyes. She smiled and said, "Yes, really." I couldn't believe it. I mean what are the chances? Yes! I could not wait to get home to tell my dad. He was in shock and couldn't believe it either. They wanted to pay for the expense of the whole trip? He had never heard of such a thing. He wanted to talk with my teacher to ensure I had heard it correctly. Once he talked with her, he gave me his blessing. To this day I still do not know if there really was a free ticket or if my teacher paid for it out of her own pocket but I'm so thankful. She allowed God to work thru her to bring one of the gifts He sent me along my journey to confirm why we should always have hope especially in situations that didn't seem possible. Thank you, Mrs. Peregrine for opening your heart and making a difference in a little girl's life, mine.

Time began to fly by, well except during the school day because it seemed time had a different dimension in the classroom seeing how it would come to a slow crawl making the day drag on forever! But in my free time, I was busy with homework, sports and being a social butterfly. I soon found myself in High School. I don't feel I ever had a set clique because I had friends in all groups from the popular to the shy crowd. I just love people, I always have and although life had its set of challenges for me things always seemed to work out. I was and am blessed. I try to always focus on the good and encourage others to do the same.

My greatest joy is being able to help someone else, to make them feel important and love when the rest of the world turns on them. It seemed at each annual Sports Banquet I would be awarded the "Miss Mental Attitude" award. I know many other people would want the MVP but for me, that was my MVP because it is who God made me to be. He gave me an optimistic outlook in life. He gave me a huge Heart to love others and a desire to persevere no matter what I face.

When we are who God made us to be and embrace the differences of others, we begin to come into understanding and can see that we are all MVPs. The only way we do not become that MVP is when we fail to live up to whom we were made to be. I want to say that again, when we fail to live up to whom we were *made to be* is the only time we do not become that MVP. A common mistake in this world is that people tend to feel they are a failure when they fail to be what others think they are supposed to be. Ask yourself, "What does God say?" Are you living the purpose He has for your life? If not, I encourage you to begin seeking Him and ask Him to guide you to your purpose. If we drive around life hoping *some day* we stumble onto the place we are supposed to be then we waste a lot of time … so why not stop and ask God for directions?

CHAPTER 5

The Flower
(Age 16)

"You therefore gird up your loins, and arise, and speak to them all that I command you: be not dismayed at them, lest I dismay you before them." James 1:17

"Sandi, would you go to Prom with me?" Dave asks as we stood in the lobby of North Newton High School. "Prom?" I say as my mind wanders off thinking about how much I would love to go but my mind quickly reminds me, *we don't have the money and I don't have the heart to ask my dad to buy a dress for me.* I would have to see. On the bus ride home I thought more about how much fun it would be and how I'd really, really like to go. Sighhhh, *I just can't do that to my dad. We don't have the money so I won't go. It's decided.* We hit a big bump in the road causing us to bounce off of our bus seats. I look out the window, *I am proud of how hard my dad works to provide for us. I mean that is not easy with 6 kids. He works so hard. It's no big deal if I don't go to Prom. I have food to eat every day, clean clothes, a bed to sleep in and two parents who love me very much even if my mom lives 12 hours away. I'm thankful. It will be okay.* My mind then shifts to the homework I have to get done. I hop off of the bus and walk a half block home to our house. I walk in the door, drop my books and run up to my room to change clothes.

I reach the top of the stairs and turn the corner into my room. I stop dead in my tracks, there in front of me is a burgundy Prom dress draped across my bed. I close my eyes and open them again to ensure I am not seeing things. It's still there, *no way!* I think. I turn to find out how this beautiful Prom dress found its way to my bed and my step mom Alice walks into my room. "I visited my cousin today and she thought one of you girls could use a Prom dress. It's been sitting in her closet for a couple of years," she says as she straightens the dress on the bed and turns her head to check her straightening work before looking up at me with a smile. My jaw drops. *Am I dreaming?* I stood there in awe and being reminded again how things do work out and how I'm being taught that there are no coincidences in life. *It seemed the moment my thoughts shifted and my Heart was in the right place, the very thing I gave up is the very thing I was given.* My Heart was jumping at the irony of how the very moment my Heart thankfully released the thought of what I wanted so much is the very thing needed to draw what my Heart desired right back to me with the force of a magnet. *How is that possible? It's like some law that defies gravity just to prove a point of how limited our comprehension truly is at understanding what is possible and how. Interesting* I ponder.

So needless to say I got to go to Prom and it was great! Things really seemed to be going well. I was active in sports (basketball and track). I was on the National Honor Society so always studying hard and of course ensuring I had time to be the social butterfly that seemed to be part of the fire within my Heart. It's who I was made to be, I love people. My sister and I were nominated for the Homecoming Court. I wanted to cry. It was such an incredible experience to be nominated and then to share that moment together as sisters. Mom couldn't be there but my step dad and she had two dozen beautiful red roses delivered to us sending their congratulations and love. It is those selfless acts of love which go right into our very Hearts forever touching them.

Before I knew it I was walking into the High School through the doors I had entered so many times before but today was different. Today is the first day of my senior year. *My senior year, I can't believe it.* The realization hit, holding my books and folder closely to my chest I walk down the hall taking everything in that I can. My heart awakens and realizes the significance this day marks ... this is the beginning of an end, the end of a very important phase of my life. My mind finally catches up with my Heart, *I'm a senior!* I stop to sort through the reality that just poured in *this is the last year we will all be together.* Sadness tries to settle into my Heart but within a matter of seconds my mind plays out all the wonderful friendships I have here in this moment, here in this place of time – the moment I anxiously wished for so many years. A tear forms in my eye and suddenly the image changes like a movie slide clicking forward. The realization sets in how quickly the time has flown by and how I want somehow to get back what I had so easily squandered away by anxiously awaiting this very day, the day I would be starting 12th grade.

Before I knew it, the end of my senior year was rapidly approaching. My senior year has been the best year yet. I am thankful though for the realization that came over me that opened my eyes to cherishing each moment of this year.

My final Track season has started. I love this sport and found that these short little legs can run. I would never be a tall, lanky model and learned to be comfortable in who I am made to be. I'm thankful for my barely 5'2" frame and Mary Lou Retton legs (so my teammates would say). The coaches are wonderful helping me do everything to get as far as I can with my sprinting. I want to win Conference, Sectional and have my eyes focused on what a dream it would be to make State. I was able to do some training with the fastest guy on the team, Mark. They pushed me to stay on his heels. So sprint after sprint I pushed harder as they cheered me on from the sidelines equipped with stopwatches in hand. My 100 yard dash times were better than they had ever been in all my years of track. Conference was quickly approaching. I was so happy and thankful for this year holding onto hope that this really could be the best year of my life. I even had an awesome dream where I was crowned princess at my Senior Prom. I think, *how cool would that be?* I feel so blessed for what an incredible year this has been.

Shortly before the upcoming Track Conference meet I woke up not feeling well. My dad encouraged me to get some rest holding to the theory that I probably had been over doing it a bit with all the training and keeping up with my studies. I stayed home sick from school that day. Well, the next day I woke up worse with a large goose egg knot that had formed underneath my skin on my neck. I showed my dad and he looked at it with a puzzled and concerned look. He made an appointment for me to see the doctor right away. A severe headache then set in that nothing would take away. The doctor ran blood work and told us that my blood counts were off the charts. They are suspecting it is leukemia. *What? This can't be happening. This is the year that is going to be different than the others. This is the year that everything is going to fall into place for me. This is my last year of High School and my only chance to pursue my track dream, NO my heart cried out! NO!!! Tears flooded my face. I just want to get back into bed. I don't feel well, I want to cry and scream out to God asking WHY? I prayed a lot and cried a lot more. Please give me a break, please God!* Hope then settled back into my heart, there is still a chance that it isn't leukemia and that I can recover to make the meet. *Hope, I need to hold onto hope,* I drift off to sleep.

I had to go back to the doctor a few more times. My blood counts had reversed showing it wasn't leukemia but the test for mono had come back positive. You've never seen a family so happy for a mono result! We were very relieved when the doctor delivered the news. I was ordered to bed rest for the next 2 to 3 weeks. Reality then set in, I saw the Conference meet slipping right thru my fingers. The thing I was holding onto so tightly, the thing my heart was focused on and all my efforts immersed in – gone in the blink of an eye, gone. I felt as if I was going to hyperventilate – what a bittersweet moment. It took me a week or so to release the bitterness that was trying to consume me. I had worked so hard for this and it was my very last chance at my dream, gone … gone!

Okay, that's enough my Heart screamed. *Focus on good things. Where's the little girl who sees the flower when the rest of the world sees all the brokenness? Where's the thankfulness that this was mono and not leukemia?* God was teaching me that we have a choice as to what road we are going to allow our minds to go down. This world was doing everything to try and take me away from the person I was made me to be. And truthfully it was doing a good job of trying to turn me into a bitter person who would give up and drown in a pool of misery. *No!!! I need to be focusing on the flower in this dark dismal moment – the bright flower. It's there if I look for it. It's there, it's always there.*

Determined to keep my mind set on good things and releasing the disappointment, I began to rest and allow my body a full chance to recover. By the time the doctor released me to return back to school I had missed the Conference meet but was learning some important life lessons. Sure for a time the Conference seemed like all that mattered in my life but the things I use to think would be the end of the world if taken away seemed to become insignificant when facing reality. I had my health back and things could have been so much worse. I was thankful.

I adjusted back to school and soon after was my Senior Prom. I had found this pretty white satin dress and picked out beautiful red roses with white flowers as my prom bouquet. I smiled when I pulled them out of the box excited to get to the Prom, see there's the flower. I was thankful my eyes were once again focusing on the good in life. We had so much fun. The crowd gathered around the stage to announce the Prince and Princess of Prom. When they called my name as Prom Princess the details of the dream I had a month ago played out again in my mind. I had completely forgotten about it and here it was happening in real life, chills formed up and down my arms at how wonderful God is and all He does to reach us. *Thank you* my heart cried out. It means so much because the class votes on who will become Prince and Princess. It wasn't the tiara being placed on my head that meant so much but the reality of why I was getting the crown. My peers cared about me, they voted for me … what an incredible gift this was and a night I will never forget.

Graduation was quickly approaching and it seemed we were all trying to hang out as much as possible because we knew how much life would change after graduation. We were nervous but excited at the same time. We were seniors and graduating! One of my best friends, John, had stopped by with one of our friends Rich. We had so much fun! We laughed until our stomach's hurt. John was an amazing person. He had so much love in his heart, was happy and always made me laugh. Rich was more shy, very kind and the two of them together could make anyone smile. They had to head out so we said good-bye and I went in to work on some homework. A short while later I heard sirens everywhere. We lived in a small town so any time you hear sirens your stomach drops because it would be someone you know either closely or have heard about them through someone else. Then that moment came that you hoped would never happen. My dad sat me down to tell me that John and Rich were killed in a head-on car accident two miles from our house. I sat there bawling. I don't think I had ever cried so hard in my life. *NO God NO! Not John and Rich, please!!!* I sobbed so hard I couldn't breathe. It kept playing out in my mind if I had only kept them there just one more minute this would not have happened, just one more minute. I became numb with pain, *this cannot be happening. It's just a bad nightmare.*

I woke up the next morning to the reality that it wasn't a nightmare. I had lost one of my best friends whom I loved dearly. I was the last one to see them alive so John's family wanted to know what he was like that night, what was his mood, what was the last thing he said. It was all so difficult but despite the pain I felt, their pain had to have been multiplied by one hundred so I was thankful I could somehow bring a little bit of comfort to them in this more than challenging time in life. The next few days were a blur. I felt like I was somewhere in between reality and some state of numbness.

It was time to head out for the funeral. It was the longest drive of my 17 years of life. As I walked up to the casket I saw the flowers all around and started to cry. I was sad and wanted to just wallow in my pity. I didn't want to come out of it but as I stood there it was a reminder that especially in a moment like this I need to look for the flower. I needed to refocus my mind on the wonderful memories of him and how many times he made me laugh. I felt blessed for the time we did have together as friends. He added so much to my life just by being who he was. He added to everyone's life who knew him. He would be missed greatly by all. The imprint he left on my heart would forever be there and silently help to push me to be the person I was made to be hoping I could somehow impact others the way he did in his short life.

John,

Thank you for being one of God's angels in helping me along my path. You are such a special soul whose life was like a gentle touch of the lips during a first kiss ... something that is so special to each person that it is never forgotten but instead holds a special place in the Heart forever.

I love and miss you,

Sandi

I was being taught to take nothing for granted and to be thankful for all I did have. I was being taught to say what I have to say so I am never robbed of the chance of ensuring someone knows I care about them. I was being taught to leave anger outside the door when it comes knocking because you never know what tomorrow brings. I was being taught to cherish the love of my family, my friends and come to understand that although miles and even death can separate us from others, unconditional Love still remains and bridges the gap of any space. We are connected through our Hearts ... each and every one of us.

CHAPTER 6

Change of perspective, Change of course
(Age 17)

"For the love of money is a root of all kinds of evil: which some reaching after have been led astray from the faith, and have pierced themselves through with many sorrows." 1 Timothy 6:10

My family lived a simple life. We didn't require much. My dad continued to instill the difference between a want and a need. I grew to realize there really isn't much we "need" in life but there sure are a whole lot of things we "want", learning the difference was yet another beautiful building block from my dad. Living a simple life and looking at things with a clear understanding of want versus need helped me to be thankful for the extras in life. I didn't *need* those extras, understanding that allowed me to see those things as gifts instead of entitlements ... a perspective that brought thankfulness for the extras instead of frustration from not having them because I never expected them in the first place. I was learning to be thankful for what I do have.

"If you continue to look at the things you don't have, you'll never be thankful for what you do have."

I didn't need the extras but I still had dreams of being successful. I wanted the American dream of the perfect husband, children, the big house with the white picket fence in suburbia and a successful career. I

33

wasn't sure how I would get it or if but had I hope that I would.

Despite all that happened in my personal life over the last year, I had to make a decision about my future. When people asked me what college I was going to attend, I hadn't really thought about it, not because of all that was happening in my personal life but, my family didn't put an emphasis on college education. Neither my father or mother had a college degree nor did any of my aunts or uncles. None of us had an extravagant life but we always had "enough" and we got by just fine. It was the world I knew and my normal at the time so I didn't have a deep desire to go to college. I wasn't brought up with the thinking that a title or college degree defined who I am but what I lived did.

Well, all that was about to change with a single appointment.

I had an appointment with the school counselor who helped students review and make decisions on many things in life including decisions that impacted our future paths like college. I had shared with him that I was thinking about pursuing Art. I loved doodling with my dad and very much enjoyed my Art classes throughout the years at school. I enjoyed learning how to draw different things and learning different techniques like perspective drawing. It was fascinating to me how everything was drawn based off of a single dot on the paper. One of my favorite teachers was Mr. Douglas. He was a kind, encouraging man who built confidence in us even when we didn't think we could draw something. I remember his thick lenses set in his dark rimmed glasses and his smile. He was a great teacher! I was excited at the thought of learning Art in a college setting.

The counselor looked at my academic scores showing my strengths and recommended I pursue business instead. He shared how there were many business positions that provided good salaries as compared to Art.

Suddenly, my eyes shifted to the success in the world and what I could obtain instead of what I could bring to the world by living who I was made to be. I hadn't yet learned that by living who I was made to be is when true success is achieved. The grades and test scores may show one thing but my Heart and how I live showed another. I love people and am happiest when I help, encourage and love others. Sure, I could pursue anything I wanted but what would really bring me joy and happiness?

Well, that is a question I know now should be asked but at that time I didn't. I had to learn that truth and this appointment was setting me on a new course to teach me that life lesson. A course taking me away from the building blocks my dad had taught me and away from living who I was made to be.

The world was selling me that by having a certain education I could make a lot of money. I would then "be successful" and as a result of my success, I would have the money to buy and do things that would make me happy. I bought into it hook, line and sinker! I would have to learn the hard way that true success has nothing to do with money.

"Money will not make you happy nor will filling your life with material things but living your purpose and

becoming all you were made to be will bring you a joy that money can never buy."

My eyes shifted to a focus of being successful in the world. My perspective changed to one of being money driven instead of purpose driven. I really wanted to start making money and soon. So how could I get education in business and get done quickly so I could start earning a living? I wasn't really interested in going away to college so I started looking into local business colleges. I found a local college where I could start right after graduating. I didn't have to wait until the fall because they had business certificates and courses that allowed you to work at your own pace. I was determined to get done fast so this was exactly what I wanted. I applied for student loans, completed the application process and was all set to begin the month after I graduated.

CHAPTER 7

Beautiful Stepping Stones
(Age 18)

"And he said, Hear now my words: if there be a prophet among you, I, Yahweh will make myself known to him in a vision, I will speak with him in a dream." Numbers 12:6

I couldn't believe graduation was over. I had made some incredible friends and hoped to stay close with them but thru the tears I shed on graduation day I knew it was an end of one journey and a beginning of a new one. Although I was super excited about starting college I was really going to miss my friends.

I had a few weeks off to enjoy summer before I started at Sawyer Business College. I could have waited to start after summer but I wanted to begin working as soon as possible. My eyes were still focused on making money, getting out on my own and buying my own car. I took the main courses I needed, scheduled them back to back, and worked hard so I could earn a business certificate within a year or so. I completed the course and with honors. I excelled in all of my classes and was ready to get into the work force!

~~~~~~~~~~

My college scheduled my first job interview for a company in South Holland, IL. I was a bit nervous because I had never driven anywhere towards the city on my own. Growing up in the middle of cornfields in a town that didn't even have a traffic light didn't exactly provide opportunities for city driving. I think I was almost more nervous about getting lost on my drive there than I was about the interview.

It was about an hour drive but the drive wasn't bad at all. My interview was with a lady named Diane. She was so nice. I had prepared my resume and listed my work experience which included corn detassling. During the interview she was impressed with my accomplishments at the college. When she saw the corn detassling job noted she was very curious as to exactly what corn detassling was. I chuckled realizing the two different worlds which we were from. Here I was from the country and she was from the city.

I explained how every summer since being 13 years old I would spend my summers getting up at 5 am, walking a mile to the bus pick up to get loaded onto the buses that would take us to the different fields around Indiana. We would file off of the buses all equipped with garbage bags over our clothes to keep us from getting soaked from the dew on the corn stalks. We would have to walk down row after row of corn pulling out the tops of each corn stalk by hand. When the sun rose in the sky, it was like a sauna in those fields and the corn stalks left their marks on any exposed skin with trails of what looked and felt like paper cuts. It was not easy work but it was great to be able to work and help pay for things I needed for school. She just smiled with a look like she couldn't imagine spending summers doing that kind of work. I could tell the fact that I did and was thankful for it set me apart from the other candidates. She smiled, thanked me for my time and said she would be in contact with me after she completed the interviews. I had a feeling in my Heart that I would get the job and I did.

~~~~~~~~~~

It was a small company with some pretty incredible people. In a short amount of time the people there became like family to me. We worked hard but had fun doing it. If you needed anything there would be someone there to help and that included in your personal lives. We celebrated birthdays, wedding showers, baby showers and holiday events together. We laughed a lot. I remember laughing so hard sometimes I would be crying. Although we were all dressed professionally in skirts, suits, etc. it was not a stuffy environment but a fun place to work. What a great job to get right out of college!

I made some incredible life-long friends at SDI and am so blessed for what those friendships have brought to my life. The relationships along the way really help us to become all we are made to be. Many people there touched my life but two people in particular had a huge influence in my life, Sandie and Ken.

I remember when I first met Sandie. She worked in marketing and was around my mom's age. She was so happy, fun and loving. We instantly felt comfortable around each other as if we had been friends for a really long time although we had just met. She quickly became like a mom to me.

Then there was Ken well what can I say other than everybody loves Ken! He has an enthusiasm and love for life that is absolutely contagious. It makes people look at him and want what he has because he is so full of life and happiness. Who wouldn't want that? I did! I wanted to know his secret but it was something I would have to learn through my own journey and the timing wasn't quite yet for me to learn it.

When I first met Ken it was similar to when I met Sandie, it was as if I already knew him and felt like he was family. I really love how that happens in life! Anyway, well Ken has always seemed so "together" and offered good advice to a sometimes pathetic, struggling, young lady ... more times than I can remember. We had a lot of laughs, great talks and all became close friends.

I felt like I had known Sandie and Ken my whole life. Our Hearts were connected for sure and as a result they could sense when I was struggling and knew exactly what to say to help me. Sandie wasn't just a good friend but brought great motherly advice. Ken was like an older brother to me and there for my spiritual guidance. We had several conversations about faith and praying, but at the time I was struggling in what seemed like every part of my life. I was focusing more on my struggles than my faith and had my ears pretty much closed to anything Ken was trying to say to get through to me. It was definitely an "it's my party and I'll cry if I want to" stage. I was having a pity party and as much as I wanted his enthusiasm for life, I couldn't see past myself to obtain it. Life had dumped on me time and time again and that is where I was choosing to focus. It wasn't where I should have been focusing.

I had many incredible things happening in my life but at the time I so easily looked right past them. I had just moved out of my dad's house and rented a place with one of my closest friends from work, Kim.

We were able to rent a beautiful home in Homewood at a more than affordable rate. I had thought of how wonderful it would be one day to be out on my own and that day was here. I was ready to spread my wings but still a little sad moving out. My dad and I were close even if we had moments where we hit heads so to speak. We had many great talks over endless cups of coffee at a local restaurant. At times I would be ready to go and dad would say, "maybe just one more cup". I would sit there thinking *how could one person drink that many cups of coffee?* Either their coffee was super good or it was a way for a dad to spend a little more time with his oldest daughter knowing that one day soon she would be out on her own. Oh my goodness and the Oreo cookie parties we would have! Countless nights we would both wake up and not be able to sleep so we'd get up to have Oreo cookies and milk. We had some of the best talks ever over cookies and milk.

Back to the incredible things happening that I failed to see at that time, forgive me God! I was driving a really nice car. I hoped one day to be able to afford one but to have it this early was more than I could have asked for, really! I was used to and brought up to drive just about anything, well as long as it was safe and legal to drive on the road, of course. We grew up in the country and as my dad would say, "We don't need no highfalutin car to get around in this there sticks." Okay, so he said it joking around and with a tone of someone from the backwoods but he meant it. He knew and was doing everything to instill within us kids that material things do not define who we are in this world. But, the world sure gave him a run for his money by trying to prove him otherwise. If I had only listened and let that that truth sink in then it would have saved me a lot of debt years later.

41

So we had a fleet of cars you could say and quite an interesting line up. One was an old Ford Torino wagon with wood panels and the same color orange that is used to so beautifully decorate the center of streets with a quaint dash pattern. Yes, I'm serious! Everyone had to know that car. I don't think even to this day I've ever seen another one exactly like it. It was unique for sure! I seriously wonder if someone gave him that car to do them the favor of taking it off of their hands. But nonetheless, it was a car and it worked especially for the wanna be Brady Bunch clan. So that car pretty much was the family car. We then had a couple of cars my dad circulated thru us kids in high school one being a Dodge Dart complete with black primer paint. I would say, *"Dad, don't you think you should paint the car one day?"* He would say, "No, it looks fine." And then there was the car I had the pleasure of driving while listening to my Whitney Houston cassette over and over. It was a 1978 white Ford LTD with gold vinyl interior. Okay, I know the car was younger than me but not by much. At that time I was so thankful to have that car and I didn't care how old it was so how could I have so quickly lost sight of that thankfulness?

My life felt empty regardless of the fact that I was surrounded by incredible people at work who were like family to me. I felt sad and lonely. I was also living from paycheck to paycheck because living on my own wasn't as easy as I thought it would be. The normal me would have found the good but instead I was looking at all of the bad. I sunk deep into that pit of misery. Despite Ken giving me pep talks I just couldn't seem to snap out of it.

Every day seemed to pull me into more and more negativity. I had a bad case of what I call the

42

"whymeez" (why me) that's for sure. But I didn't realize how bad it was until later that day. My desk was in the front office to the right of the main reception desk. The phone was ringing and ringing with no one picking it up so I answered it and wasn't happy about it. I said "Good morning, Systems Design" in a less than pleasing tone. The man on the other end of the phone sarcastically said, "Are you always that happy?" I felt a bolt of truth penetrate right thru my heart that unbeknownst to me had become hardened. I sat there with tears filling my eyes and thought *what has happened to me?*

As soon as I got home from work, I put on my pajamas and went straight to bed. I started crying and the tears wouldn't stop. I cried out asking God, "How can I be so miserable when I have so many things to be thankful for? Why do I feel so empty? Why is my life going so wrong?!"

Although I was asking for God's help, I felt somehow I had to fix things myself and had no idea how or where to start. It left me feeling helpless and with little to no hope. I thought, *God is only there to listen to me and not really do anything ... right?* I did not have any proof that He was going to help me, and so I didn't really believe He would. That thought made me cry more until I eventually drifted off to sleep.

That night I had a dream that forever changed my life. God came to me and told me that I had lost sight of my faith. He then brought Ken into my dream and told me that Ken would be helping me on my spiritual path. I was to open my mind and heart to all of it. Then it was like a movie played out in front of me and I saw all of the times Ken tried helping me but my

43

ears had been closed. I felt horrible for turning a deaf ear and being so blind to what was right in front of me. Despite hearing his words, I had not comprehended them. And I couldn't see the signs surrounding me. I realized that I needed to start listening and to find my faith again. I felt horrible looking past the help God had sent to me. I had peace and hope knowing that if anyone could help me with this, Ken could. This dream was so powerful that when I woke up I could not go back to sleep. It did not feel like a dream, it felt real. I lay there wondering in the darkness, *was it really a dream? Was that the answer? I can't wait to see Ken and tell him!*

Upon arriving at work, I hurried down the hall and barged into Ken's office. I was so excited to share with him the powerful dream I had. "You are NEVER going to believe this dream I had last night! God was in it and so were you!" I looked up and saw that he was smiling and nodding knowingly. I explained that just the night before I felt like I was at my end, at one of my weakest moments, and so I began crying out to God trying to understand why I felt so empty inside. "I know it's pathetic," I said, smiling, "but I really did have a bad night. Anyway, after I cried myself to sleep, it was unbelievable, Ken. I get chills just getting ready to tell you this. God was talking to me saying it was important for me to find my faith again. Then, next thing I knew, you were in my dream talking to me about it and helping me with whatever I needed to get back on my spiritual path. Can you believe that?"

He looked at me smiling and said, "I know."

I looked at him and said, "What?"

44

He said, "That wasn't a dream. I felt God telling me the same thing last night. He wants me to help you find your way back to Him. Isn't He wonderful?"

I had chills. I looked at Ken with an expression of amazement and disbelief as thoughts of disbelief whirled through my mind. *How in the world did he know? That is not possible! Would someone please pinch me, because I'm obviously still sleeping!?* However, I wasn't sleeping. I was fully awake and sitting right there in Ken's office. There was no question that God wanted my attention and believe me, He got it!

Ken had always talked about God with such energy, love, and joy radiating from his soul, and I really wanted to have those same feelings. I wanted that happiness, that peace, but I wondered -- *was I special enough for God to bless me with them as He had done for my spiritual friend?*

I knew Ken had prayed for me a lot. I believe that from the time he met me he felt my struggles, especially the ones relating to my faith as I was trying to follow my spiritual path. He was not surprised God used a dream to make it happen, but I was still in awe at the length God went to in order to get my complete attention. Ken understood the unbelievable things that are possible with God. "There is nothing He cannot do," Ken assured me, and I wanted to believe that but I wasn't quite there yet. I nodded as I listened to him, but in my thoughts I was wondering, *are all things really possible -- even the impossible things? How can that be?* Despite my doubts, however, I had complete trust in Ken's wisdom and his love for God, so I trusted what he shared with me.

That moment was a turning point in my life, a very important one. I had no idea that God would work through other people to help me get back on track when I was at a critical crossroad in my life. I thought there would have to be some miracle of God standing right in front of me to make it all real. But I was beginning to realize that God doesn't present Himself in a physical sense. His Spirit is in those all around us working to help us along our way, and this was truly amazing to me!

I walked out of Ken's office feeling a wonderful sense of peace inside. I felt like I could face anything as long as God was with me and I kept my mind and Heart open to the people and things God would send my way to help me. I promised myself that I would pray more often and do my best to give my troubles and my worries to God, but most importantly I was determined to trust God with my whole soul.

I was still struggling with being alone. I had friends and family in my life, but I so desperately wanted someone with whom to share my life. I had always dreamt of having a husband someday that was kind, considerate, devoted, and loving. I was still working on giving everything to God and felt selfish praying for such a person.

Ken was teaching me, however, that we can talk to God about anything, and that we need to give everything to Him. So I began to open up to God and shared what I felt my heart wanted. I had a lot to learn but these steps I was taking would teach me some valuable lessons like praying for God's desires in my Life instead of my own.

CHAPTER 8

Learning how to Pray
(Age 20)

"In nothing be anxious; but in everything by prayer and supplication with thanksgiving let your requests be made known to Yahweh." Philippians 4:6

I was praying more and more. I had prayed throughout my life, but now I realized I was still learning how to open up to God, how to get close to Him, and how to trust Him completely. I always thought I had to pray a specific way, and that it was selfish to pray for things I felt my heart needed. But I was realizing we need to be close to God, and in order to get close to Him we have to learn to turn to Him for everything!

I started talking to God as if He was my best friend, and it felt great to open up my heart and be myself without having to perform a ritual of praying the same prayer over and over, which I thought had to be done in order to heal my soul. God sent Yahushua to help us understand that we need to be close to Him. We cannot let rituals prevent us from reaching Him. He wants us close to Him. He wants a relationship with us.

How do you build a relationship with God? I have had people share with me that they want to be closer to God but they don't know how. You spend time with Him just like any other relationship. Yes, it's that simple and I have chills as I write it. Talk to Him, spend quiet time

47

with Him whether it's going for a walk, taking a bubble bath or sitting in your office. It doesn't matter where you spend time with Him what's important is that you spend time with Him.

God was teaching me that He doesn't want rituals getting in the way of our relationship with Him. Each of us has a direct line to God through prayer, and we should use it frequently! My prayers were my personal, private conversations with God – only between God and me so I really was able to open up my heart to Him.

I started talking with God about everything. I would now pray for things I needed in addition to my prayers for others. At that time I found myself praying for a man to come into my life. I prayed a checklist, a very specific one, for what I thought a perfect husband for me should be. You know the tall, handsome, smart, successful, kind, loving, devoted and treat me like a princess kind of husband.

I cried and cried. I didn't feel I was to be alone so I prayed asking for a guy to come into my life and soon. *Please God, I don't want to be alone.*

CHAPTER 9

The Party Tap
(Age 21)

"And be not drunken with wine, in which is riot, but be filled with the Spirit," Ephesians 5:18

When I moved out of my dad's house I had finally reached the age of 21. The first weekend my friend, Kim, wanted to go out for drinks and dancing. I was pretty tired and didn't really feel like it but she talked me into getting out. She knew I needed to get out of the house and out of my pity party. We went to "The Party Tap" bar located in Lansing. We sat at a table right off of the dance floor. Kim tried to cheer me up and get my mind off of things but I was a stick in the mud to say the least!

I was feeling down and trying to find something to wear that night didn't help matters. I had tried on outfit after outfit but nothing looked good on me. I had put on so much extra weight because apparently I thought I could eat away my loneliness. But what I found was the food didn't fill up my heart, it filled in my butt, my thighs, my stomach and my face. Okay, I have to chuckle here because the line from "Tommy Boy" just played out in my mind. Tommy says, "Does this suit make me look fat?" His friend says, "No, your face does." Yay, that was about right for me. It wasn't the clothes making me fat; I made me fat because I was trying to fill that void in my heart with food.

A guy approached our table and began talking to Kim. I sat there watching people out on the dance floor and then felt a tap on my shoulder. I wasn't in the best of moods and the last thing I felt like doing was talking with anyone.

I looked at Kim and she said to me, "You WANT to turn around."

I said, "No, I don't."

She said, "Yes, you do."

I said, "No, I don't."

She then gave me the older sister eye by raising her eyebrows and nodding her head towards this tall man standing behind me. We had already had a drink or two so I turned around and said, "Yes, I do."

There stood a tall, dark blonde, handsome, blue eyed man. He was dressed in a red dress shirt and black dress pants. He asked me to dance. I said, "Yes" and followed him out onto the dance floor. His name was Chris and he was very kind.

"Be sober, be watchful: your adversary the devil, as a roaring lion, walks about, seeking whom he may devour:"
1 Peter 5:8

We ended up having drinks, dancing and hanging out the rest of the night. It just so happened that his brother worked as a bouncer at that same bar so we walked over and he introduced me. And boy, I thought Chris was tall at 6'3" but his brother was 6'7". I felt like I was in the land of the giants, both of them towering over my 5'2" height!

The guy that came over to talk to Kim was Chris' best friend at the time, Gary. Chris later confessed that he was Gary's wingman. They were at our table most of the night. I could tell Gary was not Kim's type at all. It was time to get out of there. The bar was closing and they asked us if we wanted to go somewhere else. We said, "Thanks but we both have to work in the morning so we'll pass." I know Kim wasn't interested in spending any more time that night with Gary. And it didn't matter to me either way. I'm pretty sure Chris felt the same way. He was very nice and cute but there wasn't a magnetic attraction between us … no spark. He actually reminded me of a guy friend I knew in high school. Before we left he did ask for my number though so I gave it to him.

The next week he called to ask me out to lunch. We were surprised to find out our offices were blocks from each other. He had recently graduated with his Mechanical Engineer degree. He was such a gentleman and knew how to treat the ladies. He sent a dozen sweetheart roses the day before our lunch date with a note saying something like, "Looking forward to our lunch together." He was the talk of the office! The girls noticed how he was different than most men. We enjoyed our lunch date but still neither one of us seemed to be getting pulled towards one another. I was taking notice though at how different he was than other guys I had dated.

We started dating and enjoyed each other's company. We would talk on the phone a lot. Funny how in the beginning we were both opposite of who we really are inside. At that time, he was talking and I was quiet (anyone who knows me knows that is a miracle in itself!). I wasn't myself when I met Chris. I was pretty depressed. I was working on looking at the brighter things of life again but one step at a time. I was really struggling with seeing past all of the extra weight I had gained. I felt less than attractive. I wasn't feeling good about myself so wanted to blend in with the wallpaper more than I wanted anyone to notice me.

As we talked, there was one thing we had in common and that was we both wanted to have a significant other in our life. Within the last year, he had come out of a serious relationship with someone he had dated since high school. He really cared for her and the break-up hurt him a lot. Things went south after they both ventured off to college. She apparently jumped the fence thinking the grass was greener on the other side. I too had been cheated on so we each had been hurt pretty deeply. We both longed to be loved and treasured.

I was trying to understand where exactly my Heart fit in this complex universal web called love because it sure seemed like the only web I had been caught in was one where I was being served as the next meal. I was tired of being chewed up and spit out by love. In the words of Jon Lovitz, "I just wanted to be loved is that so wrong?"

Although neither of us had a pull or draw to one another, one step at a time we got to know each other. We were very opposite. I was extroverted. He was introverted. I was creative and more go with the flow. He was precise and had to have everything planned. We did both have kind, caring hearts. I kept trying to get "the friend" image out of my head because he felt so much like a friend and not a boyfriend, even from our first kiss. I remember my Heart clearly saying, "*friend*".

52

I didn't hear the words "husband" in my Heart of Hearts. The physical side perfectly fit the checklist that I had prayed, but my Heart kept speaking *"friend"*. We were there for each other and both needed healing in the love department. We both had to learn how to trust again and had high hopes that love would grow so we began to spend more and more time together.

"But he said, Yes rather, blessed are they that hear the word of Yahweh, and keep it." Luke 11:28

Despite my Heart clearly speaking "friend", we continued to date. I heard but didn't obey that Voice. A little over a year of dating we moved in together. We rented a small apartment in Steger, IL. It wasn't much but it was ours. We had started talking about marriage and began to look at engagement rings. My Heart would speak to me louder and louder, *"friend"*. I continued to ignore what I was hearing because everything on the outside seemed so perfect. And one thing I knew for sure was that God had sent Chris into my life. He was to be my friend and would be there with me thru much. I assumed at the time the role he was supposed to be in was one of husband but I never stopped to ask God because I wanted what I wanted.

My Heart was relentless, so much in fact that I talked about it to my two closest friends at the time. I told them I didn't think I should get married to Chris. He felt like a friend and not my happily ever after. Both told me I would be foolish to let this one go because no other guy was like him. They both presented all of the facts on the physical side as to why he would make a great husband. I couldn't argue the points, they were right. So, I made a decision to ignore the Voice saying *"friend"* in my Heart. I jumped in head first!

Moving in together proved to be a bit challenging. It wasn't easy getting used to each other and not being able to have your own space in a small apartment. I began to see a side of Chris I had not seen before. He was kind most of the time but not long after moving in together I saw anger coming to the surface. He had been thru a lot in his life and needed a lot of healing. He didn't talk much and would hold a lot in until it exploded like a steam screaming out of a teapot.

I'll never forget one night we went grocery shopping together at Cub Foods. I cannot remember what was said between us but suddenly the normal kind Chris I knew left his face. I saw rage come over him and his face turned very red. He hauled off and kicked me as hard as he could on my right leg. I caught myself on the grocery cart. I was devastated and tears filled my eyes. I felt so disrespected and hurt. I did not see it coming. It came out of nowhere. This certainly was not the kind, sweet man I knew.

From what I remember no words were spoken on our drive home. Tears filled my eyes. I was scared of what I saw in his face. It was NOT Chris. He is a very nice, caring man. I then heard the Voice in my Heart very clearly *"LEAVE, MOVE BACK TO YOUR DAD'S HOUSE NOW."*

"You shall walk in all the way which Yahweh your Elohim has commanded you, that you may live, and that it may be well with you, and that you may prolong your days in the land which you shall possess." Deuteronomy 5:33

We carried in the groceries and put them away. I believe Chris had gone into the bathroom. I went into the bedroom and shut the door. I pulled out my suitcase and began to pack. I had it full pretty fast. Chris then walked into the bedroom. He sat on the bed and said he was so sorry. He felt really bad for acting like that and begged me not to leave. I kept packing. He asked me to please stop packing and to stay. He was deeply sorry. I felt he really meant it so I started unpacking and decided to stay. I followed what I wanted and ignored

It wasn't long after that we got engaged on Easter. I remember having a knowing inside that the proposal was going to be on Easter and in front of his family. I was petrified and did not like surprises so I began to share that with him. He had planned on popping the question in front of his family until I ruined it by sharing how horrified I would be at the thought. Here a moment that should be cherished, I was more worried about how it was going to happen. Looking back now I can see sadly how superficial I was on some things. I was more focused on that engagement, wedding, husband and future kids than I was on ensuring the man I was marrying was the one to complete my heart and me the one to complete his.

We set the wedding date for September 26, 1992. And then the wedding planning began! I was off to the races dragging Chris and everyone else along with me. I don't think I have ever been so consumed with anything in my whole life. I was driving myself crazy so I cannot even imagine what my bridesmaids felt like. I was the epitome of the obsessed bride fully determined to have the perfect wedding down to every last detail. I spent countless hours planning that "picture perfect" wedding.

Chris and I had to begin taking classes at the church in preparation for marriage. When we first met with Father Presta, we both loved him. He was young, personable, kind and loved to smile. He began asking us questions both individually and as a couple. He looked at me and asked something along the lines of "When something good or bad happens in your life, who do you turn to first?" Without hesitation I smiled and said, "God." He looked at me and smiled really big. He hadn't had anyone respond with that answer before. I smiled back and was thankful I had found my childlike faith again.

Chris and I were married at St. Christopher's church in Midlothian three years after we met. All the planning did result in a beautiful wedding. We were young and had so much to learn especially about love but we were brought into each other's lives for a reason. We both made the decision, to walk forward on this journey together. We would be taught many lessons along the way and would weather many storms together. Neither of us knew just how soon after we said "I do" that the storms would hit the shores of our new life together.

Leap Into Future Time (LIFT)

I had no idea at the time I was being taught about the importance of obedience unto God. I did not listen to what was clearly spoken within my Heart. I thought about the facts that were right before my eyes and followed what I thought was best. God's ways were far different than my ways. It would be a long, painful lesson that took me many years to understand.

"For my thoughts are not your thoughts, neither are your ways my ways, says Yahweh." Isaiah 55:8

CHAPTER 10

Weathering the Storm
(Age 24)

*"Then Solomon spoke, Yahweh has said that he would dwell in
the thick darkness."*
1 Kings 8:12

The day after our wedding we headed for
Disney. We arrived in the afternoon and the weather
was beautiful. The skies were blue, the sun was shining
and the weather was perfect. The next day we would
wake up to gray skies and rain from morning until
night. On the fifth day we went out for breakfast at a
little café down the road from the hotel. The waitress
mentioned that she's lived in Florida all of her life and
didn't remember a time it had ever rained five days
without a bit of sunshine. I thought *that sounds about
right, the dark cloud that has always been over my head
even took the sunshine out of the sunshine state.* I
reminded myself to look for the silver lining because
there was always a silver lining.

Despite the rain, we decided to go to the main
attractions and water parks anyway. The skies were so
gray and gloomy. We still had fun going down the
water slides. The rain started to downpour but we were
already wet so what did it matter? I felt like a kid again
playing in the rain and jumping in mud puddles. The

only thing missing was my mom yelling out the door telling me to get into the house.

Well although growing up it was spoken to me more than once not to play in the rain because I would catch a cold, I didn't believe it. But here we both were with horrible colds after playing in the rain! We just wanted to go home. We were miserable so looked into flying back early but the cost to change the flights was too much money. We stayed in bed surrounded by tissues and hot cups of tea until we could get on a flight home.

Once we returned home, we went to the doctor and received antibiotics for the upper respiratory infections we had both contracted. I remember feeling really tired and thinking all of the stress of planning the perfect wedding for the last year and a half had caught up to me. Not to mention, I was trying to settle back into my work schedule after being on vacation, that is tiring in itself. Well I could make all of the excuses I wanted but my body was trying to get my attention.

About a week after I finished my antibiotic I noticed a strange rash on my legs that looked like reddish purplish dots. I had noticed it before so was thinking through if I had used anything different on my skin. I did! I had tried a new shaving cream so that's probably it. I stopped using that shaving cream but the rash was not improving. I finally mentioned it to Sandie and showed it to her. She had never seen anything like it so encouraged me to go to the doctor. I made an appointment to get it checked out.

After two hours of sitting in the waiting room, I finally saw the doctor. He examined me and said it looked like petechia.

"Peteaky what?" I said.

He repeated, "Petechia. It is a small purplish spot caused by a minute hemorrhage." I thought, *Hemorrhage? Why would I hemorrhage?* He saw the concerned look on my face and said, "No worries, it is probably just a reaction to the sulfa antibiotic you just finished. We'll run some blood work and see what we find." Off to the lab I went with multiple boxes checked under the blood part of the form and a typical scribbled doctor's signature across the bottom. They drew my blood and said it would take a few days for the results, so I was scheduled back the next week to see my doctor.

I hadn't given any more thought to it since the doctor said it was probably a reaction to the medicine, although the spots didn't improve. I started noticing them inside my mouth and even on my eyes. I left work early to follow up with the doctor. I paged through an outdated *Family Journal* magazine while I waited. I hoped it wasn't going to take two hours again just to get back there. As I looked through the magazine, there were such adorable babies in the ads! I smiled at the thought of having children one day. The nurse then called me back and the doctor came in just a few minutes later.

He asked, "Have you been in a bad car accident or anything traumatic lately?" I looked at him with a puzzled look; *what a bizarre question,* I thought.

"No, why?" I replied.

He said, "Well, your blood work came back a bit concerning. Your platelets were 10,000 and a normal range for an adult is between 150,000 – 300,000."

"Platelets? What are platelets?" I asked.

He replied, "They are a component of the blood that helps the blood to clot. Your counts are so low that you are at severe risk for hemorrhaging."

What? Did I hear him correctly? They must have my blood work confused with someone else's results. I am only twenty-four and just starting out my life ... there MUST be some mistake! This cannot be happening. God is good to me. Suddenly, all of the images of what our babies' faces might look like were quickly replaced with worry about what all of this meant ... *will I be able to have children? Is it Cancer? Will I die young?* Talk about having your life flash in front of your eyes. As I sat there looking dazed, the doctor explained what steps he would take next. "We're going to draw another blood count today to see if there was an error in the lab. I'll call you when the results are in." I thought, *phew that is exactly it, a lab error; there is nothing wrong with my blood counts.* Regardless, worry kept creeping into my mind along with the whole "What if?" scenario. I did my best to give it to God because I knew worrying certainly would not help my situation any, but this news was overwhelming. I prayed for strength.

CHAPTER 11

Waiting for the Call
(Age 24)

"casting all your anxiety upon him, because he cares for you."
1 Peter 5:7

I heard the announcement come over the work intercom that I had a call on line three. I picked up line three, "Good morning, may I help you?" It was the doctor himself, not the nurse – that was a bit startling. He said, "Your platelet count is now down to 7,000, so there was not an error in the lab." *What? No, he must be mistaken. The blood count has to be wrong.* He said, "Hello, are you still there?" I was there but didn't know what to say; this was the last thing I had expected to hear.

He said, "I'm referring you to a hematologist and you should hear from his office soon." I hung up the phone sitting there in shock. I thought *what is a hematologist?* I called Chris right away to explain what the doctor had said. He sat there silent too. It is not news either of us expected to receive nor is it how we thought we would begin our life together. I knew he would be there for me and was thankful to have him in my life.

A week later I went to my appointment with the hematologist, and while I waited for the doctor the nurse explained to me that a hematologist specializes in diseases of the blood. *Diseases?* I thought. The doctor came in and explained he was going to need to run some additional blood work and was ordering a bone marrow aspiration. *Oh my, this sounds serious -- a bone marrow aspiration.*

I never imagined I would ever have to ask this question especially in my twenties but the words blurted right out, "Do I have cancer?" I held my breath and my stomach dropped as I waited for his answer. It's one of the questions I didn't want to hear the answer to, but I knew I had to ask. He said, "It is not clear yet what is causing your platelets to be so low, but that is what we are going to find out." Not exactly the answer I wanted. I hoped he would say, "No, nothing like that." I felt worry trying to take over. *Breathe... everything is going to be okay.*

The doctor scheduled the bone marrow aspiration for a week later and explained that I should have someone drive me. He said, "Since you are so young, it may be difficult to do the aspiration on the breastbone, but that is what I would like to try first because it is less painful than the hip." *Pain, oh my now this is sounding scary.* On the drive home I kept blinking my eyes so I could see to drive through the tears. I felt sad that Chris and I were just starting our life together and that within weeks of coming home from our honeymoon; we were being faced with what appeared to be a pretty major health issue –one that could forever change our lives. I prayed for strength to understand all that we were facing. I went home to call my family and update them with the news. Everyone was trying to stay positive, but I could tell they were as scared as I was.

The bone aspiration went well. The doctor was able to perform it on the breastbone so the pain was tolerable. It seemed I would always make new friends while sitting in the waiting room so had heard stories about how painful the aspiration from the hip could be from patients who had experienced it. So I was very thankful the doctor was able to avoid the hip area for me. *Thank you, God!* It was uncomfortable, but not nearly as bad as I had expected it to be. It would take a week for the results. I was still trying to comprehend that just a few weeks ago I had just gotten married and was excited to start our new life together. Instead of worrying about how to decorate our new home or how we were going to get all of the thank-you notes written, we were worrying about the results of my next test and blood count. I kept reminding myself to focus on the silver lining no matter how big this gray cloud seemed.

I tossed and turned all night knowing that my doctor's appointment was tomorrow to review the results of the bone marrow aspiration. The waiting seemed like eternity but the day was finally here – now to just gather up enough courage to accept whatever the doctor had to say. While we sat in the waiting room, I flipped through magazines but could not focus on reading any of the articles because my mind was racing. *God, please take this worry and anxiety from me,* I prayed silently. When we heard the nurse call my name, Chris and I walked back not knowing what we would hear and how it might change our lives.

The doctor said the test came back with increased megacaryocytes; here was another medical term that meant nothing to us. He may as well have been talking to us in another language because we heard the word but had no idea what he was saying. He said the results of the bone marrow aspiration and a positive antibody against my platelets indicated that I had Idiopathic Thrombocytopenia Purpura, also known as ITP. Apparently, ITP is a rare blood disorder where the body develops an antibody against its platelets thus attacking them at dangerous levels. The doctor explained that there are a few treatments, but the first one typically involves surgically removing the spleen.

"Surgery? Why surgery?" I asked the doctor.

He responded patiently, "The last couple of months your body has failed to respond to the steroid treatment. By removing your spleen, there is a 50% chance your blood counts will go back to normal." I sat there overwhelmed at how scary just the thought of having surgery was to me. *Shouldn't you only have to have surgery if your appendix burst, or you get into some horrible accident? How is it at twenty-five I'm sitting here facing surgery, and just six short months ago I was on my honeymoon?* At that moment I realized that life is not a guarantee; it is a gift. I was learning to appreciate each day, whereas previously I had taken life for granted. I desperately wanted my normal life back.

I said to the doctor, "If it means I can get back to a normal life, then let's get this behind us." The doctor's office scheduled the pre-op visit and then surgery for a couple of weeks later.

~~~~~~~~~~

"I'm not sure. I can't find that much information at the library except a few medical definitions here and there. There isn't much information on ITP at all," I told my dad. Everyone had so many questions, but there weren't a lot of answers. My doctor found some articles

64

for me to support the statistics regarding having my spleen removed. I needed something to share with my family, wanting to give them some hope that all would work out. I needed some hope as well.

"I am scared. The whole idea of surgery just petrifies me. You heard of that guy last year that went in for ankle surgery and died on the operating table? It seems like one horror story after another," I said to Chris. He put his arms around me and gave me a gentle hug to let me know he understood, and that he was there for me. I had no idea at the time just how much he would be there for me or how many more surgeries I would be facing over the upcoming years.

I found that the thoughts of surgery were overwhelming me not only at night when I tried to sleep, but during the day too. *What if I don't pull through the surgery? What about our future? I want a family ... I just want a normal life!* I screamed silently in my thoughts. *Is anyone listening? Does anyone care?*

My surgery was about a week away, and I was growing increasingly nervous. We were all anxious ... Chris, my dad, my mom, my sister and brother – everyone. It didn't help that they saw how anxious I was about the whole thing. I was at a point where I didn't know where to turn. I felt lost and scared.

It then hit me so strongly that I needed to pray, pray, and pray some more! It was as if a guardian angel was screaming those words into my ear. Everything in my being responded with *yes, that is it!* I knew I needed to work on giving all of my worries to God. He was the only one who could take away all of my anxiety. I have always had faith, and God was no stranger in my life, but I had felt so overwhelmed with what was happening that I'd been seeking comfort and answers everywhere except for where I should have been. I took some quiet time that evening and gave God my worries, desperately pleading with Him to help me find the peace I needed. I was scared.

My dad dropped in for a visit one day. It seemed he was dropping in a lot more often since my diagnosis. I could see the worry in his face knowing his firstborn was facing such health issues. I think he just needed to see for himself that I was okay versus simply taking my word for it over the phone. He told me on more than one occasion that if he could take it all and endure it himself, he would do so, because he didn't want me going through all of this. He is an incredible man of integrity, love, compassion, dependability, and strength. I'm blessed with two great parents whose hearts are filled with love and care for those around them, especially their children. God has blessed me with a wonderful family who really loves and supports one another. I kept assuring them that I trusted God's plan. It's not easy going through all of this, but I have to trust Him.

~~~~~~~~~~

"Wow, you seem all happy and chipper. I thought your surgery was just a few days away; did they cancel it?" my dad asked. My surgery indeed was a few days away, but I was no longer worried. "Yep, sure is. It's actually six days away, but I'm not worried anymore." My dad looked at me with a puzzled look – this coming from a girl who for the last week and a half had been doing her best to put on a smile to hide how scared she was about this surgery.

66

"Dad, I had this incredible dream. I know it sounds silly, but I feel as if I have already had the surgery and all was fine. I saw myself in a hospital gown being rolled into the operating room. Next thing I know, the surgery was over, and the doctor was examining my incisions. He lifted my gown, and I saw three small bandages on my stomach. There was one right under the middle of my ribcage, another directly under my left breast at the base of my rib and another at the bottom of my ribcage on the left side." I pointed to the areas on my stomach where the small bandages were in my dream, so he knew where I meant. "Then my doctor said everything went great, and that I was going to do just fine." I told him smiling, "Then I woke up, and since having that dream I am not scared at all. I can't explain it, but I know everything is going to go great – no need to worry."

He said, "Aren't dreams strange at times? Small bandages … hmmm. You know, the doctor told you that you would have about a six-inch incision down your side. But if that dream helped you feel better about things then that is great. I'm happy to see you back to your normal, positive self. Looks like my 'Miss Positive Mental Attitude' is back."

Again, my Dad reminded me of who I've been since a little girl. He says God has given me an attitude like no other, because I seem to have hope in difficult circumstances when most would not, and I've always tried to lift the spirits of those around me. And as far back as he could remember I've always tried to save the world. "That's my girl," he said as he kissed the top of my head.

Surgery was next week, so the dream helped me give my anxieties to God, and it reminded me that He is there for me. Although I have loved God for as long as I can remember, the one thing that keeps amazing me is that once we open our Heart and Believe, God never fails to send us exactly what we need at the time we need it the most. The dream gave me the peace I so desperately needed to face surgery. It's as if God took my hand, walked with me into the future, and showed me what was going to happen (in detail). Although I was doing my best in giving my worries to God and failing miserably, He did not forsake me. He felt my struggle and stepped in to help me trust Him. The dream was so detailed and real that it removed my worries and instilled the peace He wanted for me ... the same peace He wants for each of us.

~~~~~~~~~~

This time He worked through a dream, but God works through all different avenues to let us know He is there for us. Many times He works through people. I know personally I feel blessed when He calls on me to help others. It fills my soul with such a great feeling, like what the flowers must feel when receiving rain after a long drought. Giving to others and blessing them quenches the soul. It is important that we listen to any tug of our hearts, because that tug probably means someone needs our help.

Recently I had a Heart Tug to contact a friend I had not seen since high school. We had become friends in the first grade and remained friends all the way through to our senior year. I had a dream that he was going through some troubles and needed a friend. I had not talked with him in fifteen years but felt God tugging on my Heart to call him.

I had no idea how to locate him so I went to the Internet hoping to obtain his email address. Thank goodness, I found it! I sent an email letting him know about my dream explaining that I felt he might be struggling with something. I told him that I knew it seemed a bit odd, since I hadn't talked with him in so long, but I felt strongly that I had to check on him. Within a couple of hours my phone rang, and it was him! He said he did not know what to say because he had been struggling with an upcoming divorce, his faith, and just everything in life! He really did need a friend. We talked awhile, and I explained that this is how God works and to know he was never alone. God tugs on our Hearts, so listen! I was glad I did because I was able to help a friend in need.

Here is a neat little story that tells how a young man listened to the tug on his heart despite the chance someone could think he was crazy.

A young man had been to Wednesday night Bible Study. The Pastor had talked about listening to God and obeying His voice. The young man couldn't help but wonder, *Does God still speak to people?*

After the service, he went out with some friends for coffee and pie, and they discussed the message. Several of the group talked about how God had led them in different ways. It was about ten o'clock when the young man started driving home. Sitting in his car before pulling out of the parking lot, he began to pray, "God ... If you still speak to people, speak to me. I will listen. I will do my best to obey."

As he drove down the main street of his town, he had the strangest thought: *Stop and buy a gallon of milk.* He shook his head and said out loud, "God is that you?" He didn't get a reply and so he started on toward home. But once again there came the thought: *Buy a gallon of milk.*

The young man thought about little Samuel in the Bible, and how he didn't recognize the voice, and so he ran to Eli. "Okay, God, in case that is you," the young man said, "I will buy the milk."

It didn't seem like too hard a test of obedience. He could always use the milk. He stopped at a convenience store and purchased the gallon of milk and started off toward home. As he passed Seventh Street, he again felt the urge: *Turn down that street.* "This is crazy," he thought, as he drove past the intersection.

Again he felt that he should turn down Seventh Street. At the next intersection he turned back and headed down Seventh. Half jokingly, he said out loud, "Okay, God, I will."

He drove several blocks, when suddenly, he felt like he should stop. He pulled over to the curb and looked around. He was in a semi-commercial area of town. It wasn't the best, but it wasn't the worst of neighborhoods either.

The businesses were closed and most of the houses looked dark like the people were already in bed. Again, he sensed something: *Go and give the milk to the people in the house across the street.*

The young man looked at the house. It was dark, and it looked like the people were either gone or they were already asleep. He started to open the door and then sat back in the car seat. "God, this is insane. Those people are asleep, and if I wake them up, they are going to be mad and I will look stupid."

Again, he felt like he should go and give the milk to the people in the house. Finally, he opened the door of his car. "Okay God, if this is you, I will go to the house, and I will give them the milk. If you want me to look like a crazy person, okay. I want to be obedient. I guess that will count for something. But if they don't answer right away, I'm out of here."

He walked across the street and rang the bell. He could hear some noise inside. A man's voice yelled out, "Who is it? What do you want?" Then the door opened before the young man could get away. A man was standing there in his jeans and T-shirt. He looked like he'd just gotten out of bed. He had a strange look on his face, and he didn't seem too happy to have some stranger standing on his doorstep. "What is it?" he asked. The young man thrust out the gallon of milk, "Here, I brought this to you." The man took the milk and rushed down a hallway speaking loudly in Spanish. Then from down the hall came a woman carrying the milk toward the kitchen. The man was following her holding a baby. The baby was crying.

The man had tears streaming down his face as he turned to his unexpected visitor. The man began speaking and half crying, "We were just praying. We had some big bills this month, and we ran out of money. We didn't have any milk for our baby. I was just praying and asking God to show me how to get some milk."

His wife in the kitchen called out, "I asked Him to send an angel with some milk. Are you an angel?"

The young man reached into his wallet and pulled out all the money he had with him and put it in the man's hand. He turned and walked back to his car with tears rolling down his cheeks. He knew that God still answers prayers and that God still speaks to His people.

- Author Unknown

God does still speak to His people. He speaks to us in many different ways – through dreams, tugs on our Heart, and through other people, but we have to make sure we are listening!

~~~~~~~~~~

I remember waking up groggy from the surgery, blinking my eyes as I tried to focus on anything around me. I heard a nurse softly say to me, "You did fine, dear – you are going to be okay." *What? The surgery is done, just like that? Seems like a minute ago I was being wheeled into the operating room.* I stayed in recovery for a short while and then was wheeled to my room.

The nurses carefully transferred me to my assigned hospital bed. After I'd been settled in my room for a little while and the pain had subsided, the nurse came in and said, "Since you have such a low platelet count, I need to check your dressings, honey." She lifted my gown, and when I looked at my abdomen my jaw dropped open … there on my stomach were three white bandages right where I had dreamt they would be. The doctor came into my hospital room to follow up and said the surgery went great! He shared with us that he had performed the first laparoscopic splenectomy at that hospital which only required three small incisions instead of the six-inch incision that we were all expecting. I was in awe once again at God and the ways He uses to reach us. I prayed and thanked Him for the dream He had sent me the week before. He knew just what I needed to get through this, and He had sent that message to me in a way He knew I would listen -- a way that I would know was undeniably Him.

CHAPTER 12

Trusting God's Plan
(Age 25)

"Behold, El is my salvation; I will trust, and will not be afraid: for in Yah Yahweh is my strength and song; and he has become my salvation." Isaiah 12:2

My recovery went really well after the splenectomy. The healing was so much quicker due to the fact they were able to do a laparoscopy instead of the normal six inch incision. I was thankful not to have a big scar and even more thankful the recovery was so fast. *Thank you, God!*

I remember going for the first blood count after the surgery. I was so hopeful, as was my entire family. I prayed and held onto hope that removing my spleen would put an end to the countless trips I had to make to the lab for blood draws. I had a 50/50 chance that this could put the disease into remission. We should see an increase in my platelets if it worked. I was learning more and more that none of this was in my control so as much as my mind would want me to worry, I had to trust God no matter what the results. The results were in ...

The surgery didn't work.

Disappointment settled in, my eyes filled with tears. I didn't understand and had so much hope that this would be the answer. I just wanted my normal life back. The tears then began to flow. *I trust you God even though I don't understand, please help me. Be my strength.*

My platelets remained low so I continued my frequent trips to the lab and doctor's office. It seemed my platelets were content being low but my doctor was not even close to content with the numbers. He wanted to see my platelets increase. They remained dangerously low. I knew the risks involved with such a low platelet count. It took me time to work thru the thoughts and fears of knowing I could hemorrhage internally any time with these low counts. A part of me wanted to withdraw and not leave the house but my Heart kept pressing me forward. I had to keep going and not submit to this disease. I had to keep looking up no matter what!

I went about life as normal as possible including wanting to go on vacation. I was so happy when my doctor approved a trip for Chris and me to go to Cancun. It was to be kind of like a second honeymoon since our first one was pretty much rained out.

When the trip was booked and the tickets in hand, I was like a little girl! I had only dreamt of being able to go on a vacation like this. Our family couldn't afford much so I had not been on many vacations in my life. My friends would head off to somewhere fun every spring break. I was happy for them and always so excited for them to come home and share with me what their vacation was like. A part of me so wanted our family to be able to go on those vacations but my Heart reminded me again that was a want and not a need. I was very thankful for all of the blessings even if they were mixed with challenges.

My body had adjusted to surviving with a low platelet count. I continued different treatments but failed every available option for my diagnosis. As a result, I was diagnosed with chronic refractory ITP. It was clear there was nothing more the doctors could do for me. I wanted to enjoy life the best I could and was being reminded more and more how life is not something we should ever take for granted ... ever.

We had everything packed and headed for the airport. I kept getting cramps but hoped somehow my body would hold off on the monthly thing we woman have to deal with. You girls know what I mean, it isn't something you want to have while on vacation especially a second honeymoon. I didn't know if they would have the monthly girlie supplies there so I packed plenty in my suitcase. It's always best to have too much rather than not enough, right?

Once we arrived in Mexico, I was so embarrassed. Security opened our suitcases to check the contents and there right on top were ... yep, you guessed it ... all of my monthly girlie supplies peeking out for the world to see. Okay, maybe not the world but Mexico. *I mean really? Do you have to stand up and wave hi to everyone?* I know silly for me to be having a conversation with my monthly girlie things but it was as if they had come to life and were sitting up waving at everyone. *Pulleazzzee can I get a break just once?* I shyly looked down, put my hand over my eyes and started moving my head back and forth scanning the ground for what, I don't know. I guess I thought that would somehow make things less obvious. I realize now I probably looked more like a chicken looking for its feed than I did a person trying not to draw attention to oneself. I felt like the Zinger Zapper from Dolly Madison commercials. Who was I kidding? They saw me no matter how inconspicuous I tried to be. I'm pretty sure I heard a chuckle or two from the security guy who saw them dancing around my suitcase!

We arrived at our hotel, and I had never seen a view as beautiful as the view from our 10th floor hotel room that overlooked the white sands and aqua water. I felt like I was in paradise. I have never seen anything so beautiful in all of my life. *Thank you, God for this beautiful gift.*

We got settled in our room, changed into our bathing suits and headed to the pool. We spent the day relaxing in the pool. The weather was perfect. It was truly amazing. We had gone out for a romantic dinner and were ready to go out on the town for fun and dancing! Then as soon as we were done eating, I got so tired. I asked Chris if we could go to bed early. It must have been the sun that had taken so much out of me. He was a trooper and didn't mind at all. He wanted me to rest.

Well, one night turned into six nights of me falling asleep early, and we didn't have one night out past dinner. Unfortunately for Chris this hadn't turned out to be much of a second honeymoon because I kept nodding off as soon as the sun was setting. I kept thinking *it must be the sun and heat making me so tired.*

Once we arrived back at home and had unpacked our suitcases, I was so exhausted and told Chris I was going to lie down to rest. He said, "Maybe you should call and get an earlier appointment at the doctor, because this is not like you to be so tired all of the time." *He is right. I will call to move up my appointment,* I thought as I drifted off to sleep.

My appointment was set for next week. My sister had called me at work to see how the vacation had gone. I mentioned to her how I had fallen asleep early every night. She asked, "Are you pregnant?"

I said, "What?"

She replied, "You said you have been really tired and falling asleep early every night. That's a good sign!" I thought, *nah I couldn't be pregnant ... could I?* She said, "You should pick up a pregnancy test; what harm would it do?" She was right, so I picked one up on my way home from work that day.

After dinner I told Chris, I would be back downstairs in a minute. He sat on the couch with his feet propped up on the coffee table to relax and watch a little TV. We had always talked about how much we wanted a family but with everything going on with my health, we felt we needed to wait. I took the test and walked into the bedroom to change into something comfortable. I walked back into the bathroom and couldn't believe what I was seeing. *Is that a blue line in the pregnancy window? Oh my goodness, it was very blue not even a faint blue.* I read the instructions over and over again, double-checking and checking again. There was no mistake – there was a blue line, darker than ever in the pregnancy window of the test.

As I stood there I realized I had completely pushed out of my mind what I had experienced a couple of weeks prior. The moment replayed in front of me like a movie. I can only describe it like a fluttering butterfly that unexpectedly comes to gently touch a flower and then goes on its way. Two weeks ago I unexpectedly had a message drop within my heart that something very important happened at that moment and something even more important was coming. I had butterflies, joy and love twirling around within me at the excitement of, well … I didn't know what but something! Oh my goodness, it was the moment of conception. I knew the moment the baby was conceived! Chills ran through me. With awe at this realization of truth that was announced before I held a positive pregnancy test in my hand, how could this be? *Oh my goodness I really knew the moment I conceived.* It sounded so unbelievable that I didn't mention it to anyone. I mean how in the world could I have known the exact moment of conception? God announced this baby ahead of time but it was too much for my human mind to comprehend so I pushed it right out of my mind. Yes, I have always had dreams and visions preparing me but this? This was a completely different level.

I called Chris up from downstairs. He walked into the bathroom. I held out my hand and showed him the pregnancy test. My hand was starting to shake a little from the mix of emotions that were running through me. I looked at him and said, "I'm pregnant". I saw worry written across his face. I knew how much he worried about my health and then the responsibility of becoming a father. He didn't see what I saw when I looked at him; and that is a guy who is amazing with kids so would make a great dad!

We both stood there in shock at the results that were right in front of us. We thought we needed to wait to start our family but a force bigger than us obviously had different plans. Tears filled my eyes ... I was pregnant!

CHAPTER 13

A Moment of Uncertainty
(Age 26)

"For I know the thoughts that I think toward you, says Yahweh, thoughts of peace, and not of evil, to give you hope in your latter end. And you shall call upon me, and you shall go and pray to me, and I will listen to you. And you shall seek me, and find me, when you shall search for me with all your heart."
Jeremiah 29:11-13

I called my doctor right away and shared with him that I was pregnant. He recommended I see a perinatologist. Again, I thought *speak English please doctor.* :) A perinatologist is a doctor who specializes in complicated, high risk pregnancies. I made an appointment and was feeling both excited and nervous. I've always wanted a baby but know the risks involved with my condition.

At my appointment I didn't quite know what to expect because it was my first pregnancy. I was called back to the nurse's station, asked to pee in a cup, told to ensure the lid was tightly closed, and to leave it in the small silver box with a door. I smiled and thought *alrighty then*! Now, ladies you know what I'm talking about when I say for guys this is an easy task, for a lady … not so much. I can only imagine how hysterical it would be to see myself trying to accomplish this seemingly simple test. First, it is a small cup much smaller than what we are used to normally using. Second, we can't exactly point and shoot like guys can. Third, we can't see to know when we have enough in the cup because it's underneath us, not in front of us. So, it's off to the races! The time begins of stopping and starting, checking the cup, stopping and starting, checking the cup and hoping we don't get too much and 'top off' the container leaving a big mess. I'm embarrassed to say I have done that more than once! I vote that any lady who has this mastered should get a gold medal. The things us women have to go thru, right? Well, I managed to get the urine in the cup without making a huge mess, this was a good start!

I walk out of the restroom, the rest of the world being clueless to my major accomplishment but my head is held high and my smile says it all. I did it! I then return to the nurse's station. She checks my blood pressure and weight. She writes it in my chart and I follow her to the patient room. She begins to review my health history which took some time due to my complicated health history but who am I kidding I'm still smiling from my accomplishment in the restroom just a few minutes ago. What can I say? It's the little things in life. :)

The doctor comes in, introduces himself, sits down and begins to read my health history. It doesn't seem to overly excite him. He sees complicated cases every day. He explains we need to begin with an internal exam. He then leaves the room. The nurse enters and gives me a gown. She asks me to remove my clothes from the waist down, place the gown on with the opening in the back. She definitely accentuated the words "in the back". I chuckle at the thought because I have a flash memory of the time I went to the doctor with my dad. I stepped out for a minute while he changed and when I came back in, he was sitting there with the gown opening in the front. I said, "Dad, you need to put the opening in the back." He said, "Why? It's good this way." I'm sure they have had many patients do that same thing and why she felt the need to ensure "in the back" was clear. In the back it is then!

I place on the gown and hop onto the examining table to wait for the doctor to return. He comes back in a short time and begins the exam. He says to me, "You're not pregnant." I said, "But the tests showed positive instantly." He said, "You can get a false positive. Upon examination your uterus does not have the normal changes or colors it takes on during pregnancy." I thought for a moment, *I'm not pregnant?* But the test was positive and so strong that it showed right away. I had such a strong knowing that I said, "Is there some other test that can be done?" He said, "We can do a blood test." I said, "Yes, please." So he ordered the pregnancy blood test and sent me off to the lab for the blood draw.

A couple of days later the doctor's office called me and said the blood pregnancy test was positive and to come back in a week to have another. She explained the doctor wants to ensure the counts are continuing to rise. I was happy when the test proved what I felt inside, the knowing was so strong. I felt so attached to this baby already and I don't care if it isn't much more than a few cells multiplying every day. I could feel this baby's Heart even before I could hear the baby's heartbeat on the ultrasound or before its Heart was even formed in my womb.

I love my baby.

That weekend, I went to the restroom and saw blood on the white tissue paper. My heart dropped, tears came to my eyes. *Please God, No! Please don't take my baby. I know this baby is so special, please protect it God, please.* I then took more tissue, wiped again and was so grateful that there was no more blood. I continued to pray and made frequent trips to the bathroom that day to check for more blood. Thank goodness there was no more blood, it was shed only once.

I wanted to ensure my baby was continuing to grow so waiting a week for the test seemed like forever! The week had finally passed. I had the test and the nurse called sharing the results that the pregnancy hormone levels are coming up normally. I felt a huge weight lift off of me. *Thank you, God! Thank you!*

CHAPTER 14

The Antibody Buddy
(Age 26, five months pregnant)

"Blessed is the man that endures temptation; for when he has been approved, he shall receive the crown of life, which Yahweh promised to them that love him." Jacob (aka James) 1:12

Despite my platelet counts refusing to increase, my pregnancy was going well. The ultrasounds showed a healthy normal size baby with a strong heartbeat. I'll never forget the first time I heard the baby's heartbeat. It took my breath away. I smiled somehow feeling this precious baby's heartbeat as if it was pulsating through my own blood and beating to the same drum as its mama's. The doctors monitored me and the baby closely with frequent visits to both offices. My platelets were averaging around 24,000 (again normal range is 150,000 – 350,000). At the time, I would have given just about anything to have my platelets increase. I thought it would be healthier for the baby and me but later would learn the gift of unanswered prayers.

At each blood test I would hold onto hope that my counts would come up but with each result I found myself drawing closer and closer to God because they weren't budging. I didn't understand why my counts remained low but I had to trust God knew something I didn't. Thankfully my Heart continued to remind me to look up and know there was a plan no matter how discouraging things may appear. I couldn't give up!

When I was approximately 5 months pregnant, my blood counts plummeted except this time, it wasn't just my platelets. It was my red blood cells, my hemoglobin and my hematocrit. My hematocrit crashed down to around 18 when at the beginning of the pregnancy it was 33 (normal range for an adult woman is 38 to 46). My blood counts were at critical levels.

I learned that the red blood cells are responsible for carrying the oxygen through the blood. Since my red blood cells were low, I was short of breath and not from my protruding tummy but because of the lack of oxygen in my blood. The doctor wasn't sure what was causing my counts to crash so he ran additional tests including a Coombs antibody test. The doctor explained the Coombs antibody test was a test to check for antibodies against my red blood cells.

I prayed asking God to protect the baby and get us through the pregnancy. I cried many tears not understanding what was going on and asking for strength, hope, and healing (shh). It is what would quiet my mind when it would so eagerly try to override any inner peace I had with worry. Strength, hope and healing … a prayer to shh the worry!

The test results came back positive. My body was now attacking my red blood cells. *Really? Did the other antibodies get lonely so they had to call in their friends? Ughh, please help me God.* I was then diagnosed with Hemolytic Anemia. He explained that on the rare occurrence that ITP and Hemolytic Anemia occur together, it is called Evan's Syndrome. The dark cloud continued to be over my head and the "if it is going to happen to someone, it will happen to me" odds struck again. Now I have two rare blood disorders buddying up to try and take me out. One positive about it was that Evan's Syndrome was a lot easier to say than Idiopathic Thrombocytopenia Purpura, try and say that three times fast!

On a more serious note, knowing my shortness of breath was something far more serious than a baby pressing on my diaphragm was not an easy one to get through. I was scared because all I could think about was this precious life growing inside of me. Through tears my Heart would pray, *I trust you God. I trust you. Please help me endure all that I'm facing and please protect my baby. Hold us in Your Arms, carry us through.*

The doctors increased my prednisone to 80 mg and started me on a new treatment called IV gamma globulins. The IV gamma globulins are used to help prevent infection and to decrease the severity of the autoimmune disorder. There is an increase in the chance for infection with that high of a prednisone dosage but we didn't have a lot of options. My hematocrit responded. It came up to around 27 which was still low but much better than 18. My platelets remained low at 23,000 but that is about where they had been holding so I'll take it! The baby's heartbeat remained strong and the ultrasound normal. *Thank you, God!*

I continued to work throughout my pregnancy. It helped keep my mind busy. Since I worked in an office, I didn't have to do any physical labor or anything strenuous. My friends at the office were concerned that I insisted on working but it really did help me. They were like family to me and I needed to have as normal of a life as possible. I remained focused on God with an excitement of the baby's arrival.

We were holding an even keel and for that I was thankful! Then there was a sudden dip in the waters. A storm came out of nowhere threatening to sink the boat. My counts crashed to critical levels. My platelets went down to 7,000. The doctors adjusted my prednisone and followed me closely with even more frequent blood draws. And it was a miracle that my veins were holding up so well with all of the blood draws. I prayed asking God to get us through the last trimester. *Please God, only a few more months to go. Please get us through.*

CHAPTER 15

Unanswered Prayers
(Age 26, eight months pregnant)

"Trust in Yahweh with all your heart, And lean not upon your own understanding: In all your ways acknowledge him, And he will direct your paths." Proverbs 3:5-6

I was so thankful that I had only a little over a month before the baby was due. It has been a time of great joy at the anticipation of what's coming but also fighting thru worry of what could go wrong. My faith grew much during this time because I had to completely trust God. If I looked at the diagnosis, the risks and all that was before me in this world, it would have overwhelmed me. So, I kept looking up and not on the things in this world. The excitement inside of me was strong and I had an unexplainable peace knowing that against impossible odds, everything was going to be okay. The lyrics from Bob Marley's song comes to heart, "Every little thing's gonna be alright. Don't worry about a thing …"

~~~~~~~~~~

"Honey, could you please put the crib over on that wall?" I asked Chris as I pointed to the south wall of the baby's bedroom while gently rubbing my very round, pregnant belly with my other hand. He looked at me and smiled, but I could tell he was trying to be as patient as possible because I kept changing my mind as to where exactly I wanted the crib placed. "That looks great; it is just perfect. Thank you!" I said with a big smile after he muscled it over to the same wall he had placed it on originally.

We did not want to know the sex of the baby, so we decorated the room a beautiful aqua green with a cheery, bright balloon design. The crib was filled with stuffed animals and the dresser was full of onesies, blankets, hooded bath towels, and diapers, all generous gifts from our baby shower the week before.

"Oh, look at the time. I have my doctor's appointment in thirty minutes," I said as I straightened the pillow in the rocking chair we received as a gift from my family. The doctor said it was time for me to start having weekly visits from now until the end of the pregnancy just so he could more closely monitor the baby and me, of course.

My platelet counts remained low throughout the entire pregnancy despite multiple prayers from family, friends, and local churches. I was given treatments of prednisone and IV Gamma Globulin the last few months in hopes of bringing my platelets up, but my counts would not budge. My average platelet count remained around 20,000. It seemed that with every low-platelet blood count new worries would find their way into our minds. However, we were on the home stretch now, with only five weeks to go – we were going to have a baby!

"Everything looks really good with both you and the baby. It's an exciting time, but you need to determine the date you want your baby to be born," Dr. Richman said. I knew I would need a C-Section to ensure the safest delivery for the baby and for my health, but I still had not become comfortable with the idea of picking the day our baby would be born. Isn't that part of the excitement -- not knowing the day God is going to bless you with your brand-new baby?

I told my doctor, "We'd like to have a week to think about it, if that is okay. We can tell you what we decide during my next visit," I said as I carefully inched off of the examining table using my hands to keep my balance and ensuring my feet were securely planted on the floor. "No problem; I'll plan on seeing you next week, and we will get the C-Section scheduled. We will also do the amniocentesis test to ensure the baby's lungs are developed," said Dr. Richman.

I called my mother-in-law when I got home to update her of my latest visit. Everyone wanted a weekly update on how the grandbaby was doing. "Are you sure you want to go to the next visit by yourself? I think someone should come with you," she said. I said, "No, I will be fine. I have been going every week by myself, so I'll be fine." She insisted on coming and wouldn't take no for an answer. I would soon realize what mother's intuition was all about and was very thankful she insisted on going to that visit with me.

~~~~~~~~~

"Ready to go?" my mother-in-law asked. She was right on time to pick me up for my 36-week appointment. We arrived at the doctor's office a little early. We patiently waited to be called back so we could get the amniocentesis test started. I had to do my routine urine test, blood pressure, etc., and then the nurse got me settled into a room. The doctor came in to see me. After he examined me he said, "You need to call your husband because we are having the baby today." I looked at him surprised and said, "What?" I

91

wasn't sure I'd heard him correctly. "You have developed pre-eclampsia. We need to deliver the baby soon to ensure that you and the baby are okay. Call your husband -- it is time to have this baby," he said with a smile. We were struggling with deciding what day the baby was going to be born so God took things into His own hands and decided for us. What a gift!

I called Chris at work to tell him the news. "We're what?" he said in shock on the phone. "We are having the baby, so get to the hospital as soon as possible," I said into the receiver. He dropped everything and rushed to the hospital. Although we were having a C-Section, we still had the excitement of an unexpected delivery date. We were so very thankful for that. Who would have guessed it would turn out this way? I called my mom all excited to tell her we were having the baby TODAY! She lived out of state but today was her birthday, so she was more than excited that her first grandchild was going to share her birthday.

Chris arrived just in time to spend a few minutes with me, and then they were rolling me off to the operating room. He kept holding onto my hand and didn't want to let go. I saw the worry in his face. The doctor gently removed his hand from mine, patted him on the back, and said with a reassuring smile, "She will be just fine, both her and the baby. I will come out as soon as the baby is born to give you an update."

His words were comforting helping to calm the tidal waves of reality that the surgery was high risk. It could take my life, the baby's life or both of us. My platelets were critically low so there was high risk for hemorrhage not to mention the low red cell count that reduced the oxygen in my body. My blood pressure was very high due to the preeclampsia and the protein in my urine indicated kidney involvement. Preeclampsia can affect the kidneys, liver and brain. It can cause seizures being the second leading cause of maternal deaths. So the odds again were stacked against me but I knew God had a plan. God and His Angels were going to get us through against the odds. I Believed.

Due to the high-risk nature of the surgery, Chris couldn't come into the operating room as is allowed with other C-sections. He nervously waited in the waiting room with his parents and mine. They said it would be a little while so everyone insisted on going to the cafeteria to grab a quick bite for lunch. Chris didn't want to go, but they insisted he got something in his stomach. After being down there about a half an hour he said, "I will see you guys later. I have to get back up there." His mom said to him, "Now honey, I know you are nervous, but all will be fine. Just sit and eat a bit more, and then we will all go up soon." He felt strongly that he needed to go. "I'm sorry Mom, but I feel I need to get back up there. I can't explain it. I will plan on seeing you guys upstairs," he said as he gave her a hug and kiss on the cheek.

Chris walked down the long hallway and maze of turns on his way to the elevator. Who knows why cafeterias are so tucked away in some of these hospitals. As he was turning towards the elevator he met up with a nurse pushing a brand-new baby in a carrier with a plastic dome-like top towards the elevator. He did a double take at the nametag on the side of the carrier. Was he seeing the name correctly? He leaned in to look more closely and there scribbled in black letters on a blue nametag was our last name.

His eyes got big, and he said excitedly, "That's my son!!" The nurse said smiling, "Well, congratulations, Dad, you have a healthy baby boy!" She explained to Chris that she was taking him up to the nursery. "Is there any chance I could go with you?" he said. She looked at him smiling and said, "Absolutely!"

He got on the elevator first, so he could hold the doors open while she maneuvered the baby carrier into the elevator. Chris couldn't keep his eyes off of the baby. The nurse had been in the delivery room, so she knew he had not been able to share in the experience of the live birth. She smiled as she lifted the case letting Chris reach his hand into the dome. He gently took his newborn son's tiny hand in his to hold. The love and bond were instant. Tears filled his eyes as he thanked God for this wonderful little miracle. He stood in awe at the perfect timing of them meeting in the hallway. *What a blessing being able to see my son when he's just minutes old,* he thought to himself as he wiped a tear from his cheek. It was the closest thing to being part of the delivery as possible.

I was thankful Chris listened to the Heart Tug. The family wanted him to stay there and finish eating but his Heart knew to go right then. A moment of hesitation and he wouldn't have been at the elevator at that exact moment to see his son. It's amazing how even if he didn't realize that the pull on his Heart was divine guidance, it was and it brought with it a very special gift indeed!

~~~~~~~~~

During the pregnancy, lots and lots of prayers went up for this precious baby and for my blood counts to increase. No one quite understood why my blood counts remained low especially with all of the prayers being said but through this, God taught me the important lesson of unanswered prayers.

Years later we found out that if God had answered everyone's prayers and brought my platelets to normal levels, we would have lost the pregnancy. The low count thinned my blood enough for the blood to flow to the baby, thus nurturing him in the womb. The clotting issues I had were not diagnosed until years later. At the time of the pregnancy, we did not realize what would have happened if the platelets had increased. A normal platelet count with clotting issues like mine would have stopped the blood flow to the baby causing spontaneous abortion. This was a valuable lesson on my spiritual journey teaching me to trust God's way even when I don't understand it. We were thankful for unanswered prayers and the miracle of our son's birth.

Despite the odds, Tyler came into this world healthy and perfect although the first couple of weeks were a scare. He was initially born with a low platelet count. When the doctor shared that with me, my heart sunk. It was one of my biggest fears that he would have the blood disorder I had. I remember holding him at night crying and praying so hard for God to heal him. It was hard for me to think because of me he would have the same blood issues. He was so tiny from being born a month early, he had a stint on his arm all bandaged up so they could easily draw the blood. Once he came home I had to watch him cry as they would prick his heel to get blood for the tests. The first two weeks his platelets remained low but right around 14 days, his platelets went to normal and have stayed there ever since. *Thank you, God!*

Some of my most precious moments were the private, in the middle of the night feedings with Tyler. I couldn't breastfeed due to my condition but I still bonded with my baby thru these special feeding times. I was so grateful God had gotten us thru the pregnancy, the delivery and the first two weeks bringing his blood counts to normal levels.

I love this baby so much it is beyond words. I would hold him and rock him for hours in the middle of the night, just him and me. My tears would roll down my face and fall on his precious cheeks as I prayed asking God to forever protect him and to keep him safe. I asked for God to grant me just 3 years with my son because at the age of 3 there's at least a chance he would remember his mom. I knew there was no guarantee for my life and was so thankful for the gift of our precious son. He gave me something more to fight for and even more strength not to give up. I wanted to see him grow up. I wanted him to know his mom and how much I love him. *God, please if you will give me just 3 years with my precious son I will be so grateful.*

CHAPTER 16

Test of Faith
(Age 30)

"Have not I commanded you? Be strong and of good courage;
Do not be terrified, neither be dismayed: for Yahweh your
Elohim is with you wherever you go." Yahushua (aka Joshua)
1:9

God answered my prayers and blessed me with three beautiful years with Tyler. He actually did more than that for me. My condition went into complete spontaneous remission the year after Ty was born (1995) to approximately March of 1998. Spontaneous remission is when your condition unexpectedly improves. It was another miracle for me. What a true gift it was to have a normal life back, *thank you God*!

My blood condition was doing wonderful during that time but I faced other challenges during those few years. I had two miscarriages, one in 1995 and another in 1996. It was extremely difficult to go through. We didn't quite understand the pain felt by parents who'd lost a baby through miscarriage until we experienced it ourselves. We had no clue just how much we could love or miss a baby that we never even knew physically, but that did not matter because we still held them in our hearts so closely. It doesn't matter how far along the pregnancy was, they were still our babies.

97

The second miscarriage was harder than the first because we began to wonder if we would ever be able to have another child. I personally wouldn't let go of the thought because my heart felt like our family wasn't quite complete. Chris kept assuring me that my health was more important than having a second child, and he also kept reminding me that we had been more than blessed with Tyler. He was right, and I was grateful for our baby boy, but there was still this hole in my heart. I struggled with that constantly, but I learned to ask God to help us trust Him with His plan for us. It is not always easy to trust Him, especially when being faced with things that just don't make sense, at least to us. I finally came to a place in life where I trusted God had a plan. Some day in God's time, not ours, if we were meant to grow our family, we would. My perspective began to change, and I realized that each miscarriage was a reminder to count our blessings, particularly one very special one named Tyler. We thanked God for him every day.

Ty was turning four in a couple of weeks and here I lie in bed with tears running down my face ... tears of thankfulness. The thought of the times when I would hold him at night while I prayed and asked God for just a few years with him flooded me with emotion. It's as if I walked back to that exact moment in time when I had him nestled in my arms. I am so grateful for that time, so incredibly grateful! My mind then switches over to the reality of what I am facing and the tears come stronger. *I'm sorry God, please forgive me.* These tears were tears of regret.

I found myself in the worst condition I had been since the time of my diagnosis. I stupidly, yes stupidly, made a decision that put my health condition into the biggest downward spiral to date. What happened? Vanity, pure and simple!

I was focused on staying healthy, so I worked out every day and watched what I ate, that was good. I felt great. My energy was the best it had been. I felt normal and really had minimal limitations so the sky was the limit, what a God send! But, as is common with many women, I was not happy with myself – no weight ever seemed good enough. I wanted to lose just five more pounds. Chris kept insisting that I looked great and told me frequently that I didn't need to lose any more weight. I didn't listen and kept doing everything possible to lose those last five pounds, which would not budge -- it was so frustrating! I heard about a supplement that would help boost metabolism resulting in stubborn weight loss. I started taking it and within one month my blood counts crashed to dangerous levels. The tears came stronger until I was sobbing. I put myself into the worst health spin I had experienced yet in my life -- all to lose a few measly pounds. Seriously, what was I thinking?!?

Well because of my obsession to lose 5 stubborn pounds, I became very ill. The last year had consisted of constant trips to the hospital, often in the middle of the night. I was put on multiple medications and treatments, all of which were failing miserably. We were at a point where no new treatments or options were available for my disorder – every treatment had failed. *How do I keep ending up in this same boat?* The thought was discouraging and although I knew I put myself into this health spin, I kept turning to God for my strength. I asked Him to forgive me for being so vain :(and cried out for healing. If only I could go back and do it all over again, I would have made a different choice.

My blood counts were critical and that included both my platelets and red blood cells. The red blood cells carry oxygen through your body. Since mine were critical, I had a difficult time trying to breathe. Any simple exertion was a major effort for me. I was also severely jaundiced. My skin and eyes were very yellow as a result of my body killing off red cells so fast that my liver couldn't keep up with filtering all of it out of my blood. The treatments were only making things worse for my liver which intensified things. I had horrible side effects from all of the drugs I was on. I became hypertensive (high blood pressure), developed steroid-induced diabetes, not to mention the famous steroid moon face. The prednisone caused my face to swell so much it was as if I was wearing a fat suit. It also caused me to gain a lot of weight. I had gained 40 pounds in three months' time and had gone from a size 6 to a size 14. The added weight caused more health issues for me not to mention all of the other side effects from the multiple drugs. At times I was taking in excess of 70 pills a day.

I was quickly realizing that not only was every day a gift, but every minute as well. I did my best to focus on all of the blessings in my life and not on all of the challenges. There I sat, thirty years old with a beautiful family, wishing I could feel well enough to be a good mom and a good wife, but knowing just walking to the bathroom was a major effort. I felt as if I was becoming a blood junkie, since blood transfusions were my fix to feeling well, even if only for a few hours. The blood gave me life. It provided the red blood cells I needed for the oxygen to be supplied to my body. Yes, I knew it was short-lived and only a matter of hours before my body would kill the new cells, but at least it would give me some time of feeling like I could breathe a little easier. It would give me a little energy to hug my son and read a book to him. I had so many blood transfusions that I must have the blood of all nations circulating through my veins.

I was thankful God tugged at the hearts of those people who would never meet me but so unselfishly gave me, a young wife and mother, a gift, a very important one … the gift of life by donating blood.[1]

Thank you to each of you who have donated blood. You truly give the gift of life and for that I am eternally grateful.

It seemed that with each transfusion, my body's attack on my blood cells became more and more aggressive. *God, I know you are there -- please hear my prayers. Please help me through this, but more importantly, help my family to find the strength and faith You have blessed me with. They need that faith more than they realize. It will help them understand how important it is for us to trust in Your plan, especially when we don't understand it.*

CHAPTER 17

The Best Christmas Gift
(Age 30)

"Call to me, and I will answer you, and will show you great things, and difficult, which you know not."

Jeremiah 33:3

12/24/98 - I find myself once again in the hospital at the holidays. This time is much worse than the others. There's an urgency within my heart that is deeper than anything I have felt before. I yearn to be home with my son. He's four and I miss him so much. While the rest of the world is getting stressed with everything they have to do for Christmas, that stress would be a welcomed gift over what I'm facing right now. I sit here crying out to God praying for just one more day and being thankful for each breath He is giving me. Something doesn't feel right, I can't breathe and I'm in so much pain throughout my abdomen that I can

102

hardly stand it. But I keep holding onto the hope that somehow a miracle will get me home tonight. Deep inside I know without a miracle this will be my last Christmas with my family. I need to be home, please God, please get me home! The nurses know the chances are slim to none but I will not give up hope, there's always hope, always! It seems I am that person people refer to when they say, "if it is going to happen to anyone it's going to happen to her." Just this once, I would like to be normal instead of falling into that less than 1% of the population statistic. I mean who ends up in the hospital almost every holiday? Hope, there's always hope.

Here it was Christmas Eve and I was sitting in a hospital bed, critically ill. I watched the nurses and doctors finish up their rounds going in and out of the rooms. I looked at them and wondered if they realized the gift they had in their health. They could finish their shift and go home to be with their family. They felt well so could do anything they wanted to do. They could go sledding with their kids, go Christmas Caroling, or take a drive to see the beautiful Christmas lights decorating the neighborhoods. They could sit around a fire snuggled with the ones they love. My eyes filled with tears at the gift they have that they probably don't even understand. I just want to be home with my family for Christmas.

Tyler was only 4 years old so wasn't old enough to understand what was going on, but he sensed something was wrong because his mom and dad seemed to always be at the hospital, especially around the holidays. I had spent Thanksgiving in the hospital and now again, at Christmas time, I found myself in the hospital again.

This hospital visit was different, though. The last few weeks I had progressively become worse. My stomach was extremely swollen. I had what they called abdominal distention. I felt and looked like the blueberry girl from the famous kid's book and movie called *Charlie and the Chocolate Factory*. The only difference was I didn't have a golden ticket! Instead I'd had severe pain in my abdomen for the last month. Nothing would take the pain away. I could not get complete relief from anything. The only thing that would help ease the pain a little bit was a hot bath. I would find myself taking up to three baths in the middle of the night and praying for a few minutes of relief from the relentless pain. Test after test had shown no blockages and nothing wrong, but I knew in my Heart that something was wrong. Something was so very wrong! My counts were critically low; so much that I couldn't take a couple of steps without being out of breath. I didn't have enough red cells to carry oxygen through my body. Having a thirty-year-old soul in what felt like a hundred-year-old body was difficult, at best.

I had an incredible doctor who had followed my case for some time. Despite my having a rare, challenging blood disease, he continued to care for me with different treatments available for my condition. He always encouraged me through his kindness and incredible bedside manner to hold onto hope and keep my positive outlook despite how discouraging the medical condition was that I was facing. He never discussed faith in God with me, but I knew within in my Heart that God was working through him even without words being spoken.

God also seemed to be working through one particular nurse named Heather. She had worked with my doctor for years, and it always seemed that just when I needed her most she was assigned to take care of me during my hospitalizations. She would come in and sit with me to talk and listen to me, offering me encouragement, compassion, and incredible care. She later told me she couldn't explain how during each of my hospital visits something had guided her to check the patient registry, and there she would find my name. Even when she wasn't assigned to take care of me, she would come and see me just to sit and talk with me. She would even show up to be with my family before any surgery or procedure I was about to go through. We loved her; she was like an angel, and I believe one of many earth angels that God sent my way.

~~~~~~~~~~

My doctor had ordered a special abdominal CT scan earlier that day, so I lay in my hospital bed anxiously waiting for the test. I had to drink contrast liquid to prepare for the test because it would allow the imaging to pick up all of the details, hopefully providing some answers as to what could be causing all of this pain and distention in my abdomen. The chalky liquid was in two large containers. I wanted to cry at the thought of drinking them. I could barely drink a sip of water; how would I drink all of this? I knew how important it was, so I prayed I could get it all down somehow.

No matter how much I tried, I just couldn't drink it all. It took me twice as long as instructed to drink just one container. I just couldn't drink another. I sat there discouraged with tears rolling down my face. I had to get this test done if I had any hope at all of going home to be with my son for Christmas. And, after all of this effort, I wasn't sure if the test would even show the proper results, since I wasn't able to drink all of the contrast. I prayed, *"God, please hear my prayers and get me through this."* I had this strong feeling that this could be the last Christmas I would get to spend with my family. I had never felt this ill before. I knew I had to get home somehow.

Despite not being able to drink the remainder of that horrible, chalky concoction, transport picked me up in a wheelchair and wheeled me downstairs to the radiology department of the hospital for the abdominal CT scan. The ride seemed to take forever. Sitting there, even without any exertion on my part, I felt so sick. I would try to take a deep breath and despite my best effort, I couldn't breathe. The only way I can describe it is that I felt like a goldfish gasping to fill its lungs with life-giving oxygen, but no matter how deeply it attempts to breathe, it is hopeless.

I was a fish out of water.

The technician helped me get onto the scanning table because I was too sick to do it myself. I hadn't realized just how weak and short of breath I was until I had to get out of bed. He connected the radioactive tube to my IV and started to slowly inject the dye. I felt this warm sensation go throughout my body as the dye filled my circulatory system. I lay there as the machine slowly guided me into the CT tube opening and I heard the machine announce, "Hold your breath ... Now breathe." I prayed, *"God please let there be enough contrast liquid so the doctors can see what they need to see."* The technician proudly announced that he was able to get the pictures and the images looked good! The test was behind me now. Thank God for that! As I was pushed back to my room, I knew I had to convince my doctors somehow to let me go home to spend Christmas with my family. My doctor came to check on me shortly after I arrived back into my room.

"It's obvious you are very ill and your blood counts are very low. It is not advisable to release you," the doctor said with a great deal of concern in his voice. Chris sat next to me already distraught, so I didn't want to say anything more to upset him. However, I had to somehow let the doctor know that I desperately NEEDED to be home because I sensed this was my last holiday. I didn't want to spend it in the hospital away from Tyler. I continued to plead with him while I silently prayed that God would help me get my message across and get me where I needed to be. "I am willing to take that risk. Being home with my son Christmas morning is all I want right now. I already feel very ill ... please just let me go home to have Christmas morning with him, even if I have to come right back again." He was a father, and I knew his Heart heard what mine was speaking. He agreed that if the initial scan results came back okay, then he would allow me to go home that Christmas Eve. I was thankful for his consideration. I was torn because I knew I was too sick to leave, but I also knew, with every fiber in my being, that I couldn't be apart from Chris and Tyler that Christmas.

I lay in my hospital bed watching the time tick by. It was almost 5 o'clock on Christmas Eve, and I was still waiting for the results from the CT scan. "Chris, I will be devastated if I can't go home tonight. I miss Tyler so desperately and with everything I have been through, I just want Christmas morning together. Do you think God will give that to me?" I sat there crying and praying for God to hear me. I am sure God was getting real tired of hearing all of my desperate pleas, or was He?

Chris never really had a response to questions about God; sadly the whole experience seemed to be pulling him further from God instead of drawing him to God. He believed but I found myself often concerned about what all of this was doing to him. The test of faith is not an easy one. I felt bad seeing the pain my health issues were burdening his heart with and all who cared about me. God somehow gave me the strength to endure more than I could have ever imagined but to sit and watch it devastate those I cared about so much was hard. My faith grew thru these trials but sadly it was so painful for him that it seemed more and more to push him in the opposite direction.

My doctor walked into my room. The doctor said as he smiled, "The initial results are in and nothing specific is showing so I am going to release you to go home and spend Christmas morning with your family." I got tears in my eyes for this wonderful gift. I held my arms out to hug him and said, "Thank you so much for this very special gift. God bless you!" Chris quickly gathered my stuff together and pulled the car around while an orderly pushed me to the front of the hospital so they could load me into the car. I was scared leaving the hospital, and I could sense he was too because he knew how sick I was. I knew I should not be going home, but the love I had for my family and my need to be with them for this one last holiday was so strong that I would risk anything and everything for that opportunity. There was no other choice for me. I just felt it.

The ride back was grueling; with every small bump in the road a sharp pain would shoot through my abdomen. I sat with a bucket on my lap in case I got sick, and I was just praying we could get home soon. I lay my head back on the headrest of the car seat feeling sicker by the minute. *Please, God, just get us home and get me in bed.* Every minute became a bigger challenge to breathe. Then a jolting thought struck me! *I have been so focused on Christmas morning, but what if I'm not well enough to even make it through the night? No, I have to stop that kind of thinking and trust God. I will pray and have faith that He will give me this last gift of being with my family tomorrow morning.*

Finally, one more turn and we would be in our driveway. The thirty-minute ride seemed to have taken hours, but we were finally home, thank goodness! I opened my car door and tried to step out despite Chris' pleas to sit tight so that he could come around to my side of the car and help me. I have always been too independent for my own good. I took one step and almost fell. I didn't have any energy at all. The ride took everything out of me. He gently picked me up and carried me into the house and straight up to bed. I lay there feeling so thankful to be home and continued to pray that God would get me through the night. I just kept smiling in anticipation of seeing Tyler's face Christmas morning as he beamed with excitement over what Santa had left under the tree for him. Those kinds of moments were like no other ... despite the circumstances, what a gift the doctor had given me by allowing me to be home for Christmas.

I finally drifted off to sleep, and it didn't seem like long before Tyler was at our bedside pulling on our covers saying, "Mom, Dad ... Santa came! Santa came! Come and see!!!" He was a very excited little four-year-old! Chris told him to go and sit by the tree, and we would be right down. I was too weak to walk, so he carried me downstairs and sat me on the couch right next to the Christmas tree where Tyler was running around checking out each package as if he knew how to read each tag.

Again, I was thankful for this gift on Christmas morning, and I don't mean the packages under the tree! Tyler tore through packages with a vengeance. His favorite gift that year from Santa was a toy guitar with a shoulder strap. It came with a microphone on a stand, just like a real music star would use. He loved music and loved being on center stage even more! His favorite song was "Greased Lightning." We put in the CD and watched him play his pretend guitar with gusto and sing loudly into the microphone. He kept stopping and coming over to hug me as if he knew how important this was to all of us. Despite his arms being so little, each hug felt like I was being surrounded by the love of a giant. *Thank you, God – Thank you so much for this Christmas gift,* I thought.

We watched Ty play until almost lunchtime. Since I was very ill, our families changed all of their

Christmas plans at the last minute and decided to bring the food and gifts from their homes to ours so we could spend the holiday together. We are blessed with a great family!

About the time everyone was to arrive, I felt my time was coming. I was growing weaker by the moment. I couldn't bring myself to say that to Chris, but I felt with everything in me that this was it, and I needed to get up to bed to be alone and pray. "Chris, I am not feeling very well and want to lie down awhile. Would you please take me up to bed?" I asked him. "Ty, come give Mommy a big hug and kiss, I am going to go rest a bit. I love you so very much, peanut!!" I said to him. He ran over with the toy guitar still strapped over his shoulder and gave me the best hug and kiss ever! I hugged him so tightly and did not want to let go, EVER! I had to look away because tears were filling my eyes. I didn't want him to see me upset or know what my mind was thinking, which was *what if this is the last time I get to hug my baby?*

Chris carried me upstairs and got me settled into bed. I asked him to please close the door behind him. The moment the door shut, I began to pray harder than I had ever prayed before. "*God, I trust your plan for me and am praying for the strength to endure all that I am facing right now. Thank you for this incredible gift of being with my family this Christmas morning. But, I have yet another prayer. I am very ill and need a miracle! I can feel with each minute that I am becoming weaker. Will you bless me with another chance to live? Please hear my prayers and send me a miracle. Amen.*"

At that time, I closed my eyes and waited patiently to see if my prayers would be answered. It was about 1 o'clock in the afternoon, and at that moment our phone rang. I figured it was someone in our family letting us know they were on their way, as well as checking in to see how I was doing. I heard footsteps running up the stairs and then suddenly the door was quickly opened and my husband was standing there with an urgent look on his face. "Honey, it is the doctor, and he wants to talk to you right away," Chris said. I looked at him puzzled; the doctor was calling me on Christmas day? I took the phone and hesitantly said "Hi, doctor ..."

"I just received a call from the hospital, and I do not know what made the senior radiologist pick up your films out of 150 films, but he did. He found clots going to your major organs. You need to get to the hospital *right now*," my doctor said. I dropped the phone and yelled for Chris, oblivious that he was still standing right there in front of me waiting to hear what the doctor had to say. "We have to go to the hospital right now!" I quickly explained what the doctor had just shared.

The family began filtering in the bedroom door while Chris was gathering me from bed. He yelled to them the news from the doctor and that we had to go NOW to the hospital. We hugged and kissed them all as he grabbed me, blanket and all, to place me in the car. As we were going out the door, Tyler ran over to me and wrapped his arms around my neck tight with so much love that it radiated throughout my soul.

As Chris was rushing me to the car, I looked back and saw Tyler standing in the slightly steamed glass door with big tears in his eyes. His little hands were on the glass of the door as if he was trying to reach through the door to get to me. He had a sad look that said, "Mommy, please don't leave me." I reached my hand out to him sobbing and hoping somehow he would know how very much I loved him and how I never wanted to leave him.

I didn't realize at the time that this was very symbolic of how God must feel when we are trying to reach out to Him, and how sad He must be when there is something between us and Him. We can still see Him, but the glass door, which is often our sin, keeps us from being close to Him. It blocks us, not from knowing He is there but from being close to Him until we open our hearts to Yahushua. And when we do, the forgiveness of our sins opens the door, allowing us who are God's children to be close to Him again, just as Tyler so desperately wanted to be close to me that cold Christmas afternoon.

Chris gently tucked me into the passenger seat. There wasn't much traffic, so it felt like we were at the hospital in half the time it normally took to get there. The doctor had everything ready for me to get right through the ER. Within a matter of minutes, the doctors had me on IV heparin. It thinned my blood and dissolved the clots. God saved my life that Christmas Day.

Later that week my spiritual friend Ken called to check on me. I was sharing my story about Christmas Day, and he just about dropped the phone. He said he knew something was going on because despite having a house full of people over for Christmas lunch, he felt the desperate need to pray for me intently and thus excused himself from the table to do so. We were in awe when we discovered that the time I was so desperately praying for a miracle he was also praying for the same thing for me but had no idea why, other than that spiritual tug on his heart. As we travel along on our spiritual journey, we begin to realize those Heart Tugs are unquestionably God speaking to us. These are tugs we cannot ignore and should not dismiss. Often those tugs are answers to prayers that others need, like I so desperately needed that Christmas Day. *Thank you, God, for your unfailing love and those tugs on our Hearts*!

This was one Christmas gift that was like no other! To this day I still sit and reflect on how amazing God's power really is and how blessed I was that Christmas Day. Each Christmas is a reminder that all things ARE possible with Him. I prayed, "Thank you, God, for this miracle of healing and the best Christmas gift of all -- the birth of Yahushua -- for through Him we are made whole again."

Believe in Miracles.

CHAPTER 18

How Much Can We Endure?
(Age 31)

"fear not, for I am with you; be not dismayed, for I am your Elohim; I will strengthen you; yes, I will help you, yes, I will uphold you with the right hand of my righteousness."
Isaiah 41:10

"Honey, I feel blessed that, through a miracle, a Senior Radiologist came into the hospital on Christmas day last year, of all days, and picked up MY films to save my life! What a gift that was, huh?" I said smiling. "And although my condition isn't improving much, God has a plan for me, and I can't give up," I said to Chris. He always looked at me with such amazement, wondering where I found the strength to remain so positive. He was closest to me and with me more than anyone else, so he experienced everything right along with me. He took care of me with whatever I needed, like lifting my head to help me drink water when I was too weak to lift it myself or just holding me when life got overwhelming. Despite being by my side, his faith in God was not where mine was and that weighed heavily on my heart. I would frequently pray, *God please hear my prayer, please heal me, so I can go out and do your work. Help me find a way to share the faith you have put in my heart with Chris, with my family, and with the world!*

It was challenging trying to function on a daily basis despite feeling like I had an ongoing case of the

115

flu, and it was hard not to get discouraged with treatment after treatment failing, but I was thankful for every day ... even my sick days. It was quite a roller coaster ride. It seems we would start a new treatment that would work fairly well for a period of time, and then just as all our hopes would rise the treatment would fail, crushing our hopes once again.

My faith remained constant, but I was always challenged with questions from others, such as, why is God putting you through so much? How could a loving God do this? How can your faith be so strong? I would explain that once I opened my heart and mind to God, He took care of the rest. I had peace knowing I could trust Him. The only way I can think to describe it is that I felt like I was a little girl again, learning how to swim. I can envision my dad standing in the chest-high pool water in our backyard, his arms reaching towards me gently persuading me to trust him and jump. Although I was scared, I closed my eyes, and I blindly jumped into the pool knowing he would catch me ... and that in his arms I would be safe.

Despite feeling ill, I tried to balance being a wife, a mom, and an employee, but it was difficult at times. God helped me do it by giving me strength and an incredible attitude! They say what doesn't kill us makes us stronger. If that's true, then I should be the strongest person in the universe! I would remind myself that life has to go on, and I knew I could not let this disease control me; I *had* to show it who's the boss! The doctors always seemed amazed at my attitude and strength. Numerous times they saw me pull through difficulties caused by my disease, and this didn't normally happen with most patients suffering in the same manner. My life continued to be a visual for the

Miracles of today; the things that are impossible with man but possible with God. He continued to do the impossible in my life.

I focused daily on my faith and never gave up hope. I continued to thank God for the blessing of this disease and the lives I had been able to touch along this journey. I prayed for Him to work through me to help others with true testimonies of His healing power. I was blessed with trusting God's plan for me and with the unbelievable peace He had given me that still remained. I felt there was a plan in all this ... an important one. So I would not give up and felt excited for what God was doing in my life.

My doctors tried numerous treatments, all of which failed. Where have you heard that one before? Yep, me! It sure seemed any new treatments would skedaddle as soon as they entered my body. I was beginning to feel like Edison who failed many times when trying to create the light bulb. But, he never gave up and the rest is history. I did not give up!

I continued to do what I could to educate myself on this disorder and to try to get connected with patients around the world who were facing similar issues. I had hopes of sharing some information to find the magic cure we were all so desperately seeking. My email list began to grow. I would send out updates on my condition, the treatments, the results and my experience through it all. I began to receive emails from people sharing with me how my strength and faith inspired them to get out of bed every day, and how it made the crosses they had to bear seem so insignificant. It blessed me so much to know others were being inspired seeing things thru my eyes, what a gift!

During that time, someone emailed me this incredible story. It made an imprint on my Heart forever so I want to share it with you too:

The Cross

A young woman, who was at the end of her rope and saw no way out, dropped to her knees in prayer. "God, I can't go on," she said. "I have too heavy a cross to bear." God replied, "My child, if you can't bear its weight, just place your cross inside this room. Then, open that other door and pick out any cross you wish." The woman was filled with relief and said, "Thank you, God," and she did as she was told. Upon entering the other door, she saw many crosses, some so large the tops were not visible. Then, she spotted a tiny cross leaning against a far wall. "I'd like that one," she whispered. And God replied, "My child that is the cross you just brought in."

-- Author Unknown

This story has served as a reminder to me throughout the years that even when the cross I had to bear seemed so heavy, there is always someone out there with a bigger cross to bear; therefore, I should be thankful. I found myself at a point where I would feel more than blessed just to find a treatment that would stabilize me and give me my life back. I didn't need a cure, but I wanted to be healed so I could share with the world the true testimonies of all that is possible with God.

My blood counts remained low, all of them, including platelets, red blood cells, hemoglobin, etc. I researched a treatment that looked like it might work for me. We had to keep pushing forward regardless of how small the chances were of a particular treatment helping me, and I seemed to be running out of options.

This process is called plasmapheresis; its purpose is to filter the blood in order to separate the blood cells from the antibodies by using a centrifuge. The antibodies are trapped within the filter and the filtered blood is returned to the body. The blood being returned has a reduced number of antibodies, which slows the attack on the red cells and platelets.

I would be hooked up to a machine through a two-port perma-cath that had to be surgically inserted directly into a blood vessel. One port would allow the blood to flow out into the machine and the other would return my blood to me after it had run through the centrifuge. I discussed the details with my doctors, and they agreed to try the treatment.

My appointment to have the perma-cath inserted was early in the morning with a treatment immediately following. We did the treatment and through the clear, pliable tubes the nurse thought she saw a clot in the return tube. She watched me closely afterwards but there were no signs of complications. My dad drove me home and sat with me until Chris returned home from work.

Once Chris was home, he decided to do some work in the backyard. I walked back to talk with him and noticed I could hardly breathe. I had to sit down because my pulse started racing very fast. It felt as if my heart was going to beat out of my chest. Chris yelled to my dad, "Ted, please get the phone right away. We have to call the doctor, something is really wrong." He called my doctor and was told to take me to the ER immediately! I was trying to breathe, but it was becoming more and more difficult. This was very different from the feeling I'd had when my counts crashed to critical levels. *Should we call an ambulance?* I thought. It was very scary not being able to get air into my lungs. I prayed God would help me with the anxious feelings I was having, and that we could get to the hospital … soon!

We arrived at the hospital, but I could not walk from the car to the ER. Chris pulled up, jumped out of the car, and grabbed a wheelchair. He picked me up and gently placed me in the wheelchair. He scurried me right to the triage area. As usual, the ER was packed but my doctor had called letting them know I would be arriving soon. He explained my complicated history and how I needed to be evaluated as soon as possible. The nurse was checking my vitals including checking the oxygen levels using a pulse oximeter. I saw the concern in her face as she was reading the display. She excused herself and quickly walked back to the ER area where the doctors were located. A doctor came out with her, and they brought me back immediately to be evaluated by a team of doctors. They helped lift me from the wheelchair and onto one of the small ER cart beds. They quickly changed me into a gown and started placing those sticky pads all over my chest to monitor my heart. My heart rate was extremely high and my blood pressure was not stable. At the same time, they were starting an IV in one arm and pulling blood from the other. I was still having a very difficult time trying to breathe. I could not get in enough oxygen no matter how hard I tried.

They rolled me down to have a lung CT scan. I felt so lost, alone, and afraid. I was helped onto the table for the lung scan. The technician shot the dye into my IV and then left the room while the machine talked to me telling me to hold my breath as it guided me into the scan for pictures. While the pictures were being evaluated, I sat there in that dark, cold CT scan room feeling a bit overwhelmed and scared. I prayed, sharing with God how scared I was and letting Him know how alone I felt, but I also prayed, *God, I trust your plan; please be with me and give me peace and strength to face this with You by my side!* I stared at the computer screen that showed my lung images and saw what appeared to be a hologram of Yahushua's face. I blinked my eyes a few times to ensure what I was seeing was really there, and the image did not change. I looked around the room for the technician, but he was not there. I continued to stare at those black and white images, but Yahushua's face was very clear to me. It sent chills down my spine. I did not feel alone any longer and knew that no matter what was ahead, I had to trust God.

I was brought back to the ER where the doctor who was assigned to my case was watching the heart monitor closely. He did not like the way my heart rate was sporadic, so he yelled for the nurse to inject something into my IV STAT. STAT is a medical term used for when something urgent needs to be done immediately. Within seconds, my heart rate bottomed out, and it felt as if an elephant was sitting on my chest. I could not get any air; I could not breathe! I was scared and the fear I saw in Chris' and dad's faces was too much to handle. I tried to get the words out, "I love you. Please let Tyler know how much I love him," but not a sound came out. I squeezed his hand as hard as I could, holding on for dear life as I felt warm tears rolling down my face.

I prayed to God that my prayer would be heard and that God would send me another miracle. I had faith that He would answer my prayer. By this time, all of the doctors from the ER were frantically scurrying around my bed. My husband looked like he was in shock, and I saw a tear rolling down his face. After he saw my heart rate bottom out on the monitor, I could see in his face that he knew this time truly was it ... I was not going to pull out of this one. How could I? When I glanced up I saw no activity on the heart monitor – did the connections come undone? How could it show nothing, but yet I could still see all that was going on? I lay there with tears rolling down the side of my face waiting for Yahushua to come -- either to heal me or to call me Home. I was scared at the thought of leaving my family, leaving this world, but I knew I had to trust in Him. Would I be able to hold my son again? I prayed in my heart, *I trust you God; please be with me and send me a miracle, because with you all things are possible.* Would He hear my prayer and send me another miracle?

Suddenly I felt something that is difficult to describe. It was as if God reached down from heaven and placed His hand on my head. I felt a warm, tingling feeling – almost like when your arm falls asleep, but with a warm and peaceful feeling. The tingling then went slowly from my head and worked its way down to my toes. It was as if Yahushua was taking His hand moving it over my body, from head to toe, to heal me. The tingling continued to work its way down to my toes and then I felt it leave out of my body. At that very moment, the monitors went completely normal.

The doctors were frantically looking around at each other asking, "Who did something? What did you give her? What happened?" They all looked at each other puzzled because none of them had given me any medication or done anything to stabilize me. I could tell by their facial expressions and their quiet discussions that they were searching for a scientific reason that would explain what had just transpired. No matter how much they tried to explain or make sense of it scientifically, I knew exactly what had happened ... God DID put His healing hand on me. He answered my prayer once again and sent me another miracle.

We later found out that what I had was a pulmonary embolism (a blood clot that had traveled to my lung). The blood thinner had been stopped so I could have the perma-cath inserted. This resulted in my blood being too thick during the plasmapheresis treatment. For most people, a pulmonary embolism is fatal. After learning this, we understood why the doctors were so worried and then so puzzled when I spontaneously stabilized. It was then that I thanked God once again for all He had done in my life and for giving me another miracle. He is an awesome God!

CHAPTER 19

Give Me Strength
(Age 31)

"For I will restore health to you, and I will heal you of your wounds, says Yahweh; because they have called you an outcast, saying, It is Zion, whom no man seeks after." Jeremiah 30:17

I had walked into a whole different world with this health diagnosis. Along with it, came a whole new language that made me feel like I had some sort of medical degree because of the medical lingo I could speak. I knew now what it meant when they ordered a blood test STAT. I knew a PE meant pulmonary embolism. I knew WBC stood for white blood cell. I knew what a normal CBC was supposed to look like and just how different my counts were from the norm, geez! *Why do I always have to be different?*

Anyway, I made new friends in this new, very different world ... many who had M.D. and R.N. after their names. And I even had what I'll call a new pet, a bit of a stretch of the imagination but it was one way of looking at the latest addition into this new world that I was in. I'll call him PC (short for perma-cath). He remained in place so we could try some additional plasmapheresis treatments.

Well PC lived in my jugular vein and was what the world would call high maintenance! I had to be careful not to disturb him when he slept. He had to go with me everywhere I went. He was attached to me what can I say :) Oh I crack myself up sometimes! I had to feed him saline each day and cleanse him to keep the riff-raff germs away from him. And the cleansings, let's call them his baths, were a whole big production. He didn't do anything little and got plenty of attention that's for sure. He also could not be handled by just anyone, only the cleanest of hands could come in contact with him.

Well each day we would have our special time together. I would get one of his special bathing kits out, open it up and carefully spread out the contents on the counter. I would scrub in, put on a mask, put on gloves, open the alcohol pads, fill the syringes with saline, remove the caps, swab the ends and push saline through the lines. It ensured his lines remained open and also helped keep those pesky germs away. We settled into a daily routine, one I wouldn't have imagined I would be doing had you asked me a couple of years ago but here we were spending quality time together each day.

I was going through all of this for a reason although I couldn't fathom at the moment exactly what that reason was, I had to trust there was a plan bigger than I could see. I was hopeful that this treatment would be the answer for me since so many other things had failed. There was plenty of excitement on the twists and turns, drops and near death plunges of this roller coaster so life was never boring.

We had found out not long ago that I was pregnant again (this was the 4th pregnancy). Tyler prayed often for a baby brother or sister. When I was just past 8 weeks pregnant and we heard the strong heartbeat of the baby, Chris and I shared the news with

Tyler. We showed him the ultrasound picture. He was so excited and asked if he could take the ultrasound picture to school with him to show his teacher. We said, "Yes." He was bouncing around like a jumping bean. It was cute to see him so happy and excited.

Later that week within an hour of flushing my port, I spiked a fever of 104. Chris had to rush me to the ER. This time was even more worrisome because we knew we had a pregnancy to think about as well. I became quite ill – weak, nauseated, jaundiced. The doctors admitted me to the hospital so they could determine why I was so ill. They decided to remove the perma-cath and found that it had bacteria on the tip. I told you PC was a magnet for those pesky germs. When I had flushed the lines earlier that day, the saline pushed the infection right into my bloodstream. I became septic so was transferred to the ICU. Being septic is a toxic condition resulting from the spread of bacteria in the bloodstream.

My blood disease was very active at this time and was killing off my red blood cells and platelets faster than they were being produced. The doctors were monitoring my blood counts frequently. They all became very concerned when my bone marrow shut down. They suspected a possible Parvo-B virus but were not certain. Because my bone marrow shut down, it was therefore not producing cells to replace the ones that my body was killing off. The infection was still rampant in my body. Many patients do not survive a septic infection of this kind, let alone complicating the situation with the critical state my blood disorder was in at the time.

The OB/GYN team came in to see us. They explained the seriousness of my health situation. They said that they had to treat me before the baby. I felt as if they were asking me for permission to abort my baby. I looked at them and said, "If this baby is not meant to survive then God will make that decision. We will not." I think they were shocked at my response. However, as much as I knew how serious my condition was, I could not make the decision to give up the life of the baby growing inside of me, even if it meant saving my own life.

Multiple antibiotics and steroids were going into my IV. My blood counts were critically low, so they were giving me 6 units of blood at the same time. I was praying my body would not kill the cells as fast as they were giving them to me because medically this was my only hope. The doctors told my family how serious my condition was. I lay in my hospital bed staring death in the face, again, not knowing what the next few hours would bring. I found myself praying again, even harder than before, knowing I was fighting for my life as well as the one growing inside of me. *"God, please hear my prayer and give me the strength to endure all I am facing. I believe in You and know that through You I will be healed."* I had this knowing inside that somehow I had to endure this and not give up! I didn't care that once again it was a "there's nothing more we can do" moment at the hospital. I had to look up and believe instead of looking at what appeared to be fact right in front of our eyes. A fact to the world that there was no way I could pull out of this one. But the fact in the world I am from is that all things are possible with God, all things and that included healing. I was not going to believe my time was up. God has a plan for me. He planted the seed in my heart that desires to help people, to give them hope and to let them know all that is possible when we believe and trust Him above anything in this world. This was the biggest attack on my body to date that tried to take me out of this world.

I looked past the fact that my blood was filled with infection pumping thru my veins. I looked past the fact that my bone marrow shut down and could not produce any more cells. I looked past the fact that my blood counts were critical and no one could survive on these counts for long. I looked past the fact that my body was killing the cells off faster than they could give them to me. I looked past the fact that there was nothing more that could be done for me. All of the money in the world and not a single person in the world could help me but there was One that could. And just like a little girl clings to her daddy, I clung to God with tears asking Him to protect me and heal me … asking for yet another miracle.

By the next morning, my blood counts began stabilizing, and my bone marrow started working again; thankfully, the infection was coming under control, and we were very grateful for yet another miracle from God. I felt so happy and grateful for God hearing and answering my prayer. Then the thought dropped in my heart about the baby. My happiness soon turned to worry and tears welled up in my eyes, *did my precious angel make it through this with me?*

They brought an ultrasound machine into ICU. The technician set up the machine and squirted warm, gooey liquid onto the ultrasound wand. Just as she was starting to place the wand onto my belly, I became overwhelmed with a feeling of sadness. I had a knowing the baby did not make it. I watched the ultrasound monitor and my eyes filled with tears. There on the screen was our baby. But, it was no longer an image of a healthy baby with a flickering heartbeat – instead, our baby was lifeless. The heart, although still visible, no longer flickered. My tears would not stop. We had lost the baby. My heart was heavy. I cried and cried and cried. I felt the heart and Life of this baby inside of me just like I had felt Tyler. I knew the baby was special so it felt like a part of my heart was ripped out when I saw it lying lifeless in my womb. It was a very difficult time and even more so a few days later when I was brought down to have the D & C surgery necessary to remove the baby.

We knew it would be hard to explain the miscarriage to Tyler, but we focused on the blessing of God pulling me out of another "impossible" situation. We were very thankful that I was still alive. As hard as it was telling Tyler, I was blessed with the opportunity of life and being able to be there to comfort him. I still felt in my heart that our family was not quite complete yet but trusted God's plan. After all we had been through; I knew we could not handle this on our own. We had to give it to God … completely. In His time, if we were meant to have another baby in our family, we would be blessed with one.

God works in mysterious ways. He knows the exact amount of time we each have on this planet, when we arrive and when we go Home. My precious angel's life started at the time of conception. And just like I felt Tyler's heart and spirit inside of me, I could feel this precious angel's as well … so beautiful, pure and untainted by the world. I have to wonder if the plan all along was for my angel to be in my womb, connected to me in flesh and heart, so we could cry out as one to God for the great miracle He just brought me. I have tears flowing as I write this knowing my angel is in God's Arms and was sent to me for a very important purpose. *Thank you God for Your Love and for all you do. It's true, we cannot even comprehend all you do for those who Love you. I am so thankful for the great miracle you have sent; please take good care of my precious Angel until we can meet in Heaven. I Love You.*

"but as it is written, Things which eye saw not, and ear heard not, And which entered not into the heart of man, Whatever things Yahweh prepared for them that love him—"
1 Corinthians 2:9

CHAPTER 20

Angels Amongst Us
(Age 32)

"And he said, Hear now my words: if there be a prophet among you, I, Yahweh will make myself known to him in a vision, I will speak with him in a dream." Numbers 12:6

My health continued to take a downward spiral. Due to the immunosuppressant drugs (drugs that suppress your immune system), I was contracting upper respiratory infections, pneumonia, pleurisy, and the list went on. I continued to go for frequent blood transfusions, hospital stays and countless trips to the lab. I didn't know how much longer I could go on. I hit a point in my journey where I didn't have the energy to keep fighting. My faith had not faltered but I didn't have the strength physically to fight anymore. I had peace and knew I needed to sit my family down and let them know that if God's plan was to call me Home, then I was ready to go. Looking my little son in the eyes and letting him know "it's okay if God comes to bring Mommy Home" was one of the most difficult things I've ever had to do in life. It was important that they all knew, including Tyler that I had peace and was ready. I had fought the battle as long as I could.

I was then sent a dream, a powerful one. My dad stopped by to visit us. I said, "Dad, I have to tell you about a dream I had. It was amazing,"

"I'd love to hear about your dream, honey," my dad said as he pulled his chair up closer to my bed.

"I dreamed that I was in bed and very ill. A woman walked into my room. She looked like an angel, Dad. Just her presence surrounded me with comfort and peace. She was a petite, beautiful woman with dark hair and dark eyes. She spoke to me in English, but she had a thick accent, and I couldn't tell where she was originally from. She walked over to my bed, and it was as if she was doing a healing of the hands. I woke up feeling hope that I am going to be healed. It was the most hope I have felt in a long time."

My dad just smiled and said, "Well, you know this wouldn't be the first time that God has sent you visions in a dream, so I think that is great, kiddo!" I smiled and was thankful for the strength and hope the dream had given to me. I had to keep fighting, I couldn't give up!

"... they shall lay hands on the sick, and they shall recover."
(Mark 16:18).

Many months had passed, and I was still very ill. My blood counts would not stabilize. I was going into the hospital weekly for blood transfusions because my body continued to kill my blood cells. I was on so many steroids that the side effects were overwhelming. I was failing all treatments. I had just heard about a new treatment (Antibiotic Therapy Treatment) that was helping some Lupus patients. Although I did not have Lupus, I had many of the same symptoms, and since nothing else was working, what did I have to lose? I tried to convince my doctor, but he seemed reluctant and unsure of it. I thought I would gather more research and keep pushing forward for this treatment.

I ached all of the time, so much that Carrie, Chris' sister, would give me weekly massages. She was a massage therapist in addition to her daily job at a marketing agency. It's amazing how God puts people in our lives just when we need them the most. She had moved in with us trying to save some money but ended up being there to help with Ty and anything else we needed as we made numerous trips to the hospital. My dad also felt a strong urge to walk away from a good paying job and retire early. He did not know why, but he listened to the tug on his heart. Neither one of us had any idea that he would be the one God chose to help take me to the hospital for all of the blood transfusions and treatments I would need over the next couple of years. I believe with all my heart that there are many earth angels, and I had been blessed with a few.

Carrie set up the massage table to give me a massage because I was especially hurting that day. During the massages we would talk about God and how He was giving me the strength to face all of this. At the time, she was struggling with her faith. She believed in a higher power but wasn't sure about the whole God idea. I did not know at the time that all of the things she went through with us would be the foundation she needed to build a strong faith in God. She is an incredible soul. She was often there to remind me of God's promise and undying love when I had a weak moment in my faith. It is amazing the lives that are touched and guided to God when we hold strong to our faith, especially when facing such adversity.

Shortly after my massage, I began feeling pain that started in my neck and worked its way down to my arms, spine, and then legs. I woke up Chris and told him we needed to go to the closest emergency room. I knew I couldn't make it to the University of Chicago. He drove me to the local ER, and by the time we arrived there, I was crying from all of the pain. It felt as if someone was ripping the muscles right off of my bones. It was the most excruciating pain I had ever experienced. I could not move any of my limbs because the pain was too intense. Chris lifted me out of the car and put me into a wheelchair.

I was placed on a bed in the back of the ER and left there. It seemed like forever before a doctor saw me. They would not give me any pain medicine, and it became obvious that they thought I was some druggie just wanting a pain med fix. After what seemed like an eternity, I started screaming to get Chris in there NOW!!! It took fifteen minutes of me screaming before they finally got him. I asked him to page my doctors at U of C right away and get them on the phone. He did so and then handed the phone to the doctor. I have never seen doctors move so fast or be so apologetic. They immediately started an IV and gave me strong pain medicine. They were prepping me to be transferred by ambulance to U of C.

Even the strongest pain medicine would not take the pain away. The pain of being loaded in the ambulance, the pain of being jostled in the ambulance, which felt like we were hitting every bump in the road, and then the pain of being unloaded from the ambulance was unbearable. I had no idea what was going on because I had never felt anything like this before. I was admitted to the hospital and multiple tests were performed. One of the tests showed transverse myelitis, but the pain in all of my limbs did not quite fit a particular diagnosis. Transverse myelitis is a disease of the spinal cord that generally causes weakness in the legs. I had been followed by the hematology team due to my blood disorder but was told they were going to be calling in a rheumatology team as well. The doctors were unsure of my outcome because it was not clear what was causing the pain and weakness I was experiencing.

My dad was by my side as usual. I am blessed with a great dad. As I lay resting in my hospital bed he was flipping through the TV channels when suddenly there was a knock at the door and in walked an African American gentleman in his thirties wearing a green robe like a priest would wear. He resembled my closest spiritual friend Ken thus giving me an instant feeling of comfort as he entered my room. He wore a brown, wooden cross around his neck that very much brought Yahushua to my mind. He walked over to my bed. He said, "Hi Sandi, I'm Father John. Would it be okay if I prayed with you?" I was surprised he had called me Sandi, because everyone but my friends and family called me Sandra because that was my full name shown in my medical chart. I sensed there was something different about him, but I wasn't sure what it was.

I was thankful someone came into my room to pray with me … *for* me. My fight for life was intense. I had never felt so much pain in my life. I quickly lost use of my arms and legs. It was as if my own arms and legs were pounded into a cross. Tears would flow down the sides of my face as I prayed and prayed for another miracle asking for God's help. I was very ill and yet again, the doctors did not know what was causing this pain so did not know what to do to treat me. The suffering was beyond anything I could have imagined.

He took my hand, bowed his head, and began to pray. He prayed, "Yahushua, please heal Sandi. You have heard her prayers and her cries for healing for some time now so that she can go out and do Your work … to go and share the wonderful blessings You have done in her life, the true testimonies to You. Heal this girl and let her begin the work You have planned for her." He continued on with his prayers, and the more he prayed the more I was in awe at what God was doing. I opened my eyes and stared at him, in awe at what I was hearing. He was praying the same very personal, private prayers that only *I* had prayed to God. No one else would have known those prayers, yet there he stood in my room asking God for the same things my very soul was seeking. He finished with "Amen" and left telling me that he hoped God would heal me soon so I could begin helping others.

When he left, I looked to my dad and said, "I don't even know what to say right now." I explained how Father John had just prayed my very personal prayers that only God would have known. My dad just shook his head in awe saying, "There is no doubt you are one of God's special children. I don't know what to say either." My mom has always told me the same thing. I think both of my parents had witnessed the true power of God so many times through my journey that they felt there was a special plan for me.

Soon the nurses came in to check on me. We mentioned Father John's visit and how much it meant to me. They looked at us puzzled saying they did not know of a Father John and had not seen anyone come in or out of my room. My dad and I looked at each other with amazement and got chills down our spines. Was Father John real or was he an Angel sent by God?

I had progressively worsened throughout the night. I could feel my legs but I couldn't move them. I felt incredibly weak as if complete atrophy set in. The next day my dad came back to visit me, and we heard doctors talking outside of my room. We could hear the rustling of the papers in my chart and their discussion of my rare case. The door opened and in walked a woman doctor. Just the sight of her brought me comfort and hope. She had the presence of an Angel. My eyes filled with tears, and I turned to my dad and said, "Dad, that's her, that IS her!! That is the woman in my dream, the one that healed me." My dad's jaw dropped, and he said, "She is just like you described her from your dream." We both just stared at her in awe.

She approached my bed as I stared at her with tears streaming down my face. She introduced herself and began to talk with me. I knew I had to tell her about my dream. It was one of my strongest Heart Tugs yet. I said, "I am very sorry to interrupt you but you were in my dream. You're an Angel sent to heal me." She just smiled, and we shared an instant spiritual bond. She is different from any other doctor I had ever met. She seems to bring the combination of medicine and spirituality to her treatment just by her presence. She introduced herself as Dr. Nadera Sweiss. I asked where she was from, and when she replied "Jordan," I was in awe! She is from the Holy Land -- of all the places in the world.

We discussed my case in detail. I shared with her the details of the Antibiotic Therapy that I was so desperate to try. She researched it and agreed it was worth a shot. She also wanted to try a new drug (Cell

Cept) they were using on transplant patients. Although there were no medical findings to support it being used in anyone with my condition, she felt guided to try it in my case. She did not ignore that tug on her heart, the one we need to learn to trust and listen to despite our hesitations, despite our occupation, sometimes in defiance of any human logic.

Prior to Dr. Sweiss walking into my room, I had hit rock-bottom. There were no known medical treatments remaining for me to try. There appeared to be little hope but I trusted God's plan and remembered the dream He had sent me … a dream of hope. After all when we hit rock-bottom there is nowhere to go but up, right? I knew to hold strong to my faith and not give up. She started a regimen of the Cell Cept and Minocin (the Antibiotic Therapy). Within a couple of months my blood counts had stabilized for the FIRST time in years and I had regained complete control of my arms and legs. I was in awe, once again, at all that is possible with God. He sent me another miracle! My faith was strengthened so much knowing God stayed true to His promise … He did not forsake me.

CHAPTER 21

Perseverance ... Finding Inner Strength
(Age 32)

"... confirming the souls of the disciples, exhorting them to continue in the faith, and that through many tribulations we must enter the Kingdom of Yahweh.'" Acts 14:22

The treatments Dr. Sweiss introduced put my blood disease into remission. It was great to feel good again! I honestly had no idea how bad it really was until I felt well again. The only way I can describe it is like having the worst flu you can imagine and having it last for years instead of days. I was so thankful to be getting my life back. *Thank you, God. Thank you! Thank you!*

Day by day, we were able to get back to some normalcy in our lives. That included the busyness life sends each of us whether it is running our children around for different sports activities, completing a major project at work, helping care for a parent, or being there for a friend in need. Life happens, doesn't it? It felt good to be part of life again; a life where I could take more than a few steps before I had to sit down and catch my breath. Soon Chris, Tyler, and I would once again do things that normal families could do, things most families either take for granted or don't take time to do because they are caught up in that busyness of "life."

We were able to take long walks along a wooded path in late fall when the air was cold enough to bundle up but not so cold that we needed hats and gloves. It was nice to breathe that wonderful, brisk fall air and take in the beauty of God's handiwork. We were surrounded by multiple colors of bright yellow, vibrant orange, and fiery red leaves displayed on the trees hugging the path on which we walked. It felt like heaven to me! I definitely had learned to appreciate the little things in life.

The condition of my blood disease was fantastic! Every blood count continued to show normal results. I stared at the first few test results because I felt like I was dreaming – it seemed too good to be true. Even so, it WAS true, my blood counts were normal – every part of them! I had the energy and health to be a wife, a mother, a daughter, a sister, and a friend again. I had been given a new lease on life.

I could be me! Being a type "A" personality, trust me -- that was saying a lot! I could do the big things as well as the little things that we all too often take for granted. I thanked God every day for giving my life back to me.

If only those who have good health would realize what a special gift God has given them. They have the freedom to go after their dreams. It is easy to take life for granted, especially living in a country where anything is possible. Seeing "In God We Trust" inscribed on the back of a U.S. dollar bill suddenly brought new meaning to me. The United States represents freedom just as trusting in God brings freedom. If we trust in God, we can have freedom with endless possibilities. This freedom represents the peace and happiness He wants for each of us.

We all have the vision to see the good in our lives that God surrounds us with all of the time, but we have to have our eyes *open* in order to see it. Only we are in control of whether we are going to be happy today or not. It is easy to blame others for our unhappiness, but if we focus on the blessings in our lives, then we are one step closer to God. Our focus then becomes the good that's in our lives; we no longer focus on the negativity, which can easily rob us of the happiness God wants for each of us.

~~~~~~~~~~

My blood counts remained stable and I was so thankful! I then began to notice a strange pain in my right hip. It was almost as if my lower back or tailbone was somehow out of alignment, which sent shooting pains into my hip. I made an appointment with the doctor because I knew I needed to have it evaluated. It seemed the pain was progressing pretty quickly. The initial doctor dismissed it as nothing, but my Heart was telling me it *was* something. I kept pushing for testing and treatment until my regular doctor recommended I see an orthopedic surgeon for a consultation.

Throughout the years I had learned to listen to that tug on my heart because for me, it was definitely God speaking to me, whether directly or through an angel speaking on His behalf. It is incredible what happens when we start paying attention to exactly how often we are being guided to do something. The signs are there – we should not ignore them and what God is trying to tell us. If we regularly ignored stop signs and stoplights in traffic, barely missing getting hit, how many times would we be fortunate enough to cruise through unharmed? More often than not, harm would befall us, which we could've spared ourselves had we paid attention to the stop sign in front of us. Likewise, please make the decision to be safe with God and stop when His spirit tugs at your heart to not move forward, but definitely press on when you sense He is telling you to go!

~~~~~~~~~~

I was able to get an appointment with one of the top orthopedic surgeons at the University of Chicago. What a blessing that was! It was awesome how God perfectly lined up just the right people to help me along my journey. The doctor evaluated me, ran some tests, and then reviewed the results with us. We were surprised at the diagnosis. He said I had a condition called AVN (Avascular Necrosis). "What?" I said as I looked at him baffled, trying to understand a medical term that once again sounded like another language to me. He explained that it is a condition where the bone tissue dies due to lack of blood supply. They believed the prednisone could be the main contributor. All I knew was that it was already some months ago when I'd had that episode of excruciating pain in my bones and so finding a treatment as soon as possible was critical.

He explained, "Well, I have good news and bad news. The good news is that although the left hip shows the AVN too, we have a 50% chance of saving that hip by doing a hip core decompression surgery." I sat there staring at him trying to comprehend what he was saying. My mind wandered, thinking, *My left hip? What do you mean my left hip? Only my right hip had the pain.* He continued, "The bad news is that your right hip has advanced AVN so you will most likely need a

142

total hip replacement. You are young, and we do not like to perform total hip replacements unless we absolutely have to do them." *Did he just say total hip replacement? What does core decompression mean? I am only thirty-two years old!* Many things were flashing through my head. I was very active and loved to workout, run, ski, and skate, plus, it was only a few months ago that I had just gotten my life back! The thought of a total hip replacement seemed discouraging, but I reminded myself that I could get through this … I knew I could. I said to myself with resolve, *God will give me the strength! Look at all I have already faced. He will get me through this storm too.*

He said, "Since things seem to be progressing pretty quickly, we need to schedule the core decompression as soon as possible. It will be a difficult surgery recovery because you will not be able to put weight on the leg for six weeks." He explained, "The core decompression is a technique where we drill into the bone to remove a portion of it, which allows increased blood flow by stimulating growth of new blood vessels."

Just the thought of such a procedure made me blurt out, "Ouch!" as I cringed in imaginary pain. Chris reached over and grabbed my hand to ensure I knew he would be there to help me, and to once again carry the weight of things that seemed difficult to bear, just as St. Christopher was said to have done for Yahushua. Next to God, Chris was my hero! We met with the nurses and scheduled the pre-operative appointment as well as the surgery.

I will not deny that worry and doubt tried to creep into my heart. I was determined to focus on my blessings. My blood counts were still normal -- that was huge! I cannot imagine what would have happened if I had still been in a critical state when I developed AVN. How could I have dealt with being so sick on top of the horrible pain this condition brought? I was quickly learning that God truly does only give us what we can handle. I was determined to face this new set of challenges with optimism, just as I had faced all of the others. I pushed the worry out and replaced it with more trust in God. My heart felt good because I knew God would not forsake me. Medically there was only a fifty percent chance of saving my left hip, but I had God on my side, so even if there was only a one percent chance, nothing, and I mean NOTHING, was impossible with Him. I felt strongly there was a plan, and I knew to be patient and trust Him.

~~~~~~~~~~~~

The core decompression surgery went great! I was sent home on crutches with strict instructions not to put any weight on the leg. We lived in a beautiful two-story home that had many stairs leading up to the level where the bedrooms were located. This was the kind of lovely home I had only dreamt of having some day as a young girl. It's amazing the blessings that are brought into your life once you open your heart to God.

When I hobbled through the front door on my crutches, the stairs were the first thing I saw. I thought, *Wow, it is going to be awesome that soon I will be flying up and down those stairs again -- woo hoo!* I settled in on the couch for the day and figured I would camp out downstairs for a few days until my hip was doing a little better. Tyler ran over to hug me and welcome me home. I had really missed him! He was now six –years old and being quite a trooper with all he had to go through with his mommy.

The next six weeks were not easy doing everything on crutches, but I managed. My shoulders really started to hurt. The doctors contributed the pain to the length of time I had spent on the crutches. My right hip hurt more and more. It was bearing my entire weight, which aggravated the condition even more. By the time the six weeks had passed, my right hip was in unbelievable pain and my shoulders were a close second.

I went in for my six-week evaluation, and we were pleased to hear that the core decompression was a success. The fifty percent chance ended up being a hundred percent with God on my side. We were able to save the hip! I couldn't believe how many blessings came mixed in with all of the challenges. No matter what challenge was staring me in the face, I found myself becoming excited, just waiting to see what God was going to do next. The stronger my belief, the more God delivered His promise. I was amazed over and over again at all that was possible. To think it had been there the whole time, and all I had to do was Believe. And, yes, at first that meant blindly leaping, but it was worth the jump! It was definitely worth the jump!

Over the next few weeks my right hip continued to deteriorate to such a degree that at the follow-up appointment the X-ray showed that the hip had collapsed. The bone was jagged, which explained why I would scream in pain whenever I tried to stand up. It was tearing into the surrounding muscles. Despite being on pain pills, the pain was so intense that when I tried to move around, such as to get into bed or go to the restroom, it seemed nearly impossible to do. Tears would roll down my face because it hurt so much – just constant, searing pain. Even lying down without moving a muscle was extremely painful. I could no longer dress myself or do simple things I had once taken for granted, like shaving my legs. I was determined to get through this latest ordeal, so I continued to try to do things for myself, but each time the jagged bone would send sharp, stabbing pain through my hip like I'd been stabbed. Soon I found myself in a wheelchair and no longer able to walk.

My shoulders continued to worsen and soon started hurting as much as my hip. The doctors evaluated the pain and determined it wasn't from the crutches but instead was also from the AVN, which had now advanced rapidly and taken hold in my shoulders. I was only in my thirties and my bones were deteriorating more every day. I was facing bi-lateral shoulder arthroplasty surgery; a surgery that replaced the ball part of the shoulder with a metal shaft. I sat in shock when the doctor told me all my joints were dying at once. I had to make a decision as to whether I should have my shoulder surgeries done first or my right-hip replacement. I was a young mom; how was I going to take care of my family?

My shoulders were bad. I could barely move them and could no longer dress myself, but more sadly, it was impossible for me to hug Tyler or Chris. It was as if there was an invisible spacer between my elbows that would not allow my arms to reach together. It was difficult to raise a glass in order to get a drink, and I felt bad not being able to help with Tyler or anything else that needed to be done around our house. I had become helpless, and I so desperately wanted to hug my baby!

It was difficult having my normal life back for a few precious months only to have it taken away again, but I had faith, and I knew with God I could do this! Despite my discouragement, it was amazing how once my faith was in the right place, my entire perspective changed. Many years ago Ken tried telling me that, but I wasn't always listening. Had I understood the peace and strength it would bring, I would have opened my mind and heart sooner instead of feeling sorry for myself when something bad would happen to me.

I could only think this is what David must have felt like when he faced Goliath. David's faith was unshakable, especially after God had delivered him from the lion and the bear. David was a young boy, yet he stood up against this strong giant. I knew that if he could defeat a giant with a stone to prove there was a God, I could also withstand all I was facing. I prayed that my triumphs could be testimonies proving that there is a God -- a God who still does miracles, even today.

Each day was a challenge, but with God, I was ready to fight whatever battle I needed to fight. The simplest tasks seemed monumental at times. I could have easily become discouraged knowing I couldn't get myself a drink of water, bathe myself, brush my teeth, dress myself, play with my son, or take care of my family – but who was on my side? Yes, God was! The pain and all I faced wasn't easy but I kept fighting thru hoping for the chance to help others, even just one person, so they can have the same Faith and Love God has put in my Heart … then every bit of this suffering would be worth it. The same peace and strength are out there for each of us, people just need to know it is true and I was praying my Life would be that visual for God. I had to stay strong!

Although once a very independent woman, I was learning to surrender because I could not do it on my own any longer. I continued to turn to God for strength. I knew that, despite how difficult things were at the time, He would be with me through each surgery and that someday I would be free of pain once again. We go through things for a reason. There always is a silver lining to the gray clouds, but we have to look for it and never give up hope. I felt strongly about this one, and although I did not understand the reason for all of these surgeries at the time, a year later it would become very clear to me.

~~~~~~~~~~

Finally, it was time to have my hip replacement. The doctors made it clear it was going to be a hard recovery with daily physical therapy needed. My mom came to stay with me for a month. She knew it would not be possible for Chris to take that much time off from work, and helping me bathe wouldn't exactly be something my dad would do. What an angel she is! I was so thankful she was unselfishly offering to help us for an entire month. I really have been blessed with incredible parents, and actually, an incredible family.

I was ready for surgery and before they wheeled me down to the operating room, I said to my family, "Guys, don't be so worried. It is awesome that my blood counts are stable for the surgery, and God is right here with me. Trust in His plan and know it will all work out." They each leaned down to hug and kiss me before I was wheeled off to the operating room for my right hip replacement. I knew the risks I was facing. I had an extremely complicated history with a medical chart a few inches thick to prove it. The doctors had to stop my blood thinner for each surgery, which was extremely risky. When I am not on blood thinner, I ran the risk of throwing a blood clot; a clot that could result in taking a wife and mother away from a young family. In addition, any trauma could trigger my disease to go into a hyper-state causing another attack on my cells. This would lower my blood counts, thus adding more risk. There also was increased risk of a post-operative infection due to a suppressed immune system from the medications I was on. We would then have to re-introduce the blood thinner with the risk of bleeding out if things were not healing inside as expected. Despite all of these risks, I had so much hope and peace even in this scary situation. Soon we were in the ice-cold operating room and the nurses were moving me from the cart to the operating table. Within minutes they had me hooked up to different IVs. They placed a mask over my nose and mouth and asked me to count backwards from 100. I started counting "100, 99, 98, 97, 96 …" and I drifted off to sleep.

Chris was very nervous in the waiting room, as was the rest of my family. My brother, who does not like hospitals at all, was there too. He knew how serious this surgery was going to be for me. They all knew what could easily happen in that operating room. Chris, mom, dad, and my brother found a table off to the far left side of the surgery waiting area to get settled in for what could be many hours. Despite my assurances to them that all was going to be okay, they were worried. Before my surgery I had prayed that somehow I would be able to figure out a way to take the faith and peace from my Heart and put it into theirs. I found myself praying often for those around me, asking God to open their minds so they could have the same incredible peace and strength He had blessed me with.

Heather, my earth angel nurse, knew I was having surgery, so she came down to check on them. She was so sweet and kind, quite an incredible girl. She knew exactly what we needed to get through all of this scary medical stuff. She was single and had recently broken up with her boyfriend. A couple of weeks prior to my surgery, I had mentioned to her that my brother was also single, and maybe she should consider going out on a blind date with him. She said, "You have a brother?" Since Mike did not like hospitals, he had never come to visit. She did not like the idea of blind dates, so I wasn't sure how they would meet but knew if they were meant to meet, they would. Later, I was surprised to hear my brother was going to be there for the surgery and I thought maybe, just maybe, they could meet that way. It wasn't the most ideal setting, but at least they could meet each other without the awkwardness of a blind date.

Chris stood up when Heather walked in. She saw Mike and thought he was really cute, so she immediately felt nervous. I heard later that she was acting like a giddy school girl and even hid behind Chris! My brother just smiled and knew he *had* to see her again. Heather sat with my family awhile to ensure they were okay and kept checking with the nurses to see how I was doing. She wanted to ensure I was going to be okay, because the surgery was running longer than normal. She helped my family so much that day. I was thankful God worked through her to bring them the support they needed while they sat worried and scared in that hospital waiting room.

150

I made great progress the first couple of weeks after my hip replacement surgery. I was excited to go back to the surgeon for my follow-up visit so I could share all I had accomplished in physical therapy. I had just gotten past the point of feeling constant pain and saw the light at the end of the tunnel! During my follow-up appointment I was surprised to hear from the doctor that I had developed a hematoma in my right hip, and I would have to go back in for surgery to have it removed. A hematoma is when your blood collects in a certain area and is usually clotted. I had noticed a rather large lump on my right hip, but since the hip felt good, and therapy was going great, I thought it was normal swelling from the surgery. My mom had mentioned she didn't think it looked quite right. There was that mother's intuition again … a heart tug! A couple of weeks ago the thought of going right back in for surgery would've been overwhelming. It compares to what a woman might feel after just giving birth to a baby and then finding out two weeks later she would have to deliver another one. It would not be on the top of her "things to do" list! However, sitting in that doctor's office, I felt strong yet again; I knew I could do this with God on my side. Something good was going to come of all of this … something really good.

The hematoma removal went well, and I was back to therapy in no time at all. Soon I was walking with a walker, and then a cane. Yes, it was unnatural being in my early thirties walking around the neighborhood with a walker, but that was nothing. I was thankful that God had brought me through a major surgery safely, and that I could walk again. I was no longer in a wheelchair, and that was a huge gift!

151

Despite the odds, I had made it through yet another surgery safely and with great results.

One Christmas afternoon, not long after my surgeries, I found myself scurrying around running late for a Christmas gathering. *Darn it! I forgot to wrap a gift!* I thought. I walked upstairs to our walk-in attic to get the Christmas paper and gift tags. I picked up the Christmas tags and didn't realize the package was open. Next thing I knew, 200 Christmas tags were scattered all over the floor. It was worse than a 52-card pick-up! It was 200 small Christmas tags, come on! I got down on my knees to pick up the tags, feeling very frustrated. I had no time for this! What tough luck it was dropping all of these tags! It then hit me ... I got a tear in my eye and thanked God for the ability of being able to bend down to pick up the tags that busy afternoon – because just one year ago I wasn't even able to walk! Something that would normally be a nuisance in a busy Christmas season was a special gift to me. It served as a reminder of all that we tend to take for granted and all we should be thankful for. *"Thank you, God, for this mess of 200 tags in front of me and the ability to bend down to pick them up!"* I started singing the words, "I'm dreaming of a White Christmas" in my head as I gathered up the Christmas tags, smiling with a thankful heart!

~~~~~~~~~~~

My two shoulder surgeries were next. Each surgery was a few months after the one prior. It was a difficult year of pain, surgery, recovery, and physical therapy but all very important to my spiritual journey. I went through five surgeries that year. Looking back now my Heart overflows with thankfulness as to where I was and where God has brought me to today. During that time life as I knew it was stripped away from me. I lost the ability to walk when the pain was so excruciating in my hip that I was confined to a wheelchair. I couldn't feed myself, dress myself or bathe myself. I couldn't hug my baby because the pain in my shoulders and deterioration of my joints wouldn't allow me to lift my arms. My eyesight also deteriorated so I went from having perfect 20/20 vision to seeing a fog everywhere I looked. I had developed cataracts in both eyes (yes, in my early 30s) so eye surgery was added to my long list of surgeries helping ensure surgeons received a paycheck. We all have a role in the circle of life don't we?

After my eye surgery I remember sitting in Dr. Garber's office. He was beginning to start the exam and my eyes were filled with tears. I had looked down and could see the clear lines of tile with crisp black lines. I said, "Dr. Garber thank you so much for helping me see again." It was such an incredible gift and yet again another thing I had taken for granted ... the ability to see. Before the surgery everything was a blur and those lines before the surgery looked like nothing more than smudges of grayness. I had been given my eyesight back! Sure I had to adjust to using reading glasses and corrective lenses to see distance (my eyesight was deteriorating like my health) but I was thankful the fog had lifted. I could see again!

~~~~~~~~~~

Leap Into Future Time (LIFT)

January 2013 - I have an eye doctor in my local area that has followed me for years. I was long overdue for my exam so was hoping my eyesight was doing okay. I hadn't noticed any problems and actually was seeing things better somehow. After the doctor completed my exam, he sat looking at me with a state of wonder and if his jaw could have hit the ground it would have! I asked with a curious smile, "What?" He said, "Well, eyes don't normally get better. They either stay the same or they get worse." He paused as if he was trying to comprehend what is fact right before him. He continued, "Your eyes have improved 3 whole steps in the right eye and 2 whole steps in the left eye. You don't even need a corrective lens anymore." I said, "Thank you, God! I then looked at him and said, "Your look reminds me of when I was having coffee with my Dad. The sun was shining in on my eyes and you would have thought my Dad had seen a ghost. He looked at me with shock and said, 'how did your eye color change? You were not born with that eye color.' I said Dad I told you God is fully transforming me. I told him God was just joining Heaven (my left eye turned blue) and earth (my right eye turned greenish gold, brown)." I chuckled at the thought of my Dad's expression that day and now the doctor's expression today for yet another miracle. The doctor looked at me and said, "God sure is doing something with you." I said, "Yes, He is!"

The smile didn't leave my face knowing the Miracles are continuing in my life. *Thank you, God! Thank you for all You continue to manifest in my life.* He never ceases to amaze me. So if you're in need of a miracle, don't you let anyone tell you that it will never happen because ALL THINGS ARE POSSIBLE WITH GOD, ALL THINGS! I am living proof of that truth and multiple times! So you pray for that Miracle and don't ever give up believing in the things which you cannot see ... because that is the true walk of faith.

We walk by faith and not by sight.

~~~~~~~~~~

The Gift in it all ... All of the suffering I endured during those times leading up to my surgeries, during my surgeries and after my surgeries taught me how to appreciate and be thankful for the things in life that I had taken for granted too easily. I learned the precious gift of a hug when I could no longer hug. I learned the precious gift of walking when I could no longer walk. I learned the precious gift of seeing when I could no longer see. *Thank you God for pulling me through things I could have never done alone.*

These challenges strengthened my faith and taught me many very important lessons. I also learned how important it was during those times of difficulties to turn towards God and not away from Him because He got me through every time even what I call the "impossibles" of this world.

With Him, I was able to persevere through it all -- the pain, the discouragement of not being able to hug those I love so much, and knowing I had to give up my pride by becoming completely dependent on someone else. I truly felt blessed by having this disease, not sorry for myself – my eyes were opened to all God was doing to teach me, and it was a powerful revelation! It had taught me to persevere, and most importantly, it taught me that I could face anything with God on my side. He continued to prove to me over and over again the things that were possible with Him.

CHAPTER 22

Bringing Two People Together
(Age 32)

"And Yahweh Elohim said, It is not good that the man should be alone; I will make him a help meet for him.'" Genesis 2:18

Let's go back a bit so I can share what happened with Mike and my nurse angel Heather. Well, in my brother's words, his meddling sister decided she needed to play matchmaker one more time for her brother because her previous attempts had been so successful -- actually, make that unsuccessful, but I didn't give up easily! Mike is nicknamed Pickle. When Ty was little, he couldn't say Uncle Michael so instead it came out as Uncle Mickle. One time it slipped as Uncle Pickle and we all started laughing. My family is awesome! Every time we get together we are in stitches laughing hysterically, especially at Mike. He is the baby of the family and is one of the funniest people I know! Mike's little three-year-old nephew unknowingly gave him the nickname that would stick forever -- Pickle!

Back to the story ... being the matchmaker I loved to be, I told Mike about this wonderful nurse at U of C who had suddenly become single. He said to me, "Suddenly? What -- did she off her ex or something?" I was cracking up laughing already. I told him that he might be able to meet her at my upcoming hip surgery.

156

With Mike's love for hospitals, he was all excited to get to meet a girl there. Not exactly! So as I went into surgery, Mike waited in the waiting room with our entire family present, I might add, for when he would meet Heather. I asked Mike to share his story, so in his own words, documented by Pickle, here goes:

In walks this stunning woman. She says hi to Chris and immediately asks him for a hug. *Wonder if my sister knows about that?* She then did not let him sit down and continued to use him as a shield. I did not get a good look at her, but I could tell Chris had received a perfect haircut. I managed a smile and a hello to Heather and even stood to shake her hand. What a Casanova move, a handshake. After she left, I was grilled by my family asking me, "Why didn't you talk to her?" Like meeting a girl for the first time is something you want to do with your whole family there.

Time passed and Sandi informed me that Heather was coming to her house, and that I should come down after work. Again, my sister Susan is there with her family so it is another instance of Heather meeting me in front of my whole family again. Not my style! I rush home after work so I can go to Sandi's. To my disappointment I got there thirty minutes after Heather left. Sandi got on the phone and convinced Heather to come back. She finally agreed and showed up later in the evening.

We sat around the table and talked, although I did not say more than two words to Heather that night. The highlight was when I had to excuse myself to go use the bathroom. Little did I know the toilet upstairs did not always flush properly, and Tyler (who was about 7 or 8 at the time) had no problem announcing to the entire house that "there was poopy left in the toilet." Just as my embarrassment was at its highest point, Susan came to the rescue and took the blame. Whew – couldn't let Heather think I actually have a normal functioning bowel.

Chris started a bonfire outside, so we all gathered around the fire to talk. I think I sat next to Heather, but I still did not talk to her. When the evening came to an end she left before I could work up the courage to walk her to her car. After she left, I was again put on the spot by my sisters as to why I did not talk to her, walk her to her car, or even get her number. I asked Sandi to ask Heather if it was okay for her to give me her number. I could contact her on my own time with less of an audience.

I called Heather during the week, and we made plans to go out. Something came up, and we had to delay our first date. I suspect this was due to her other boyfriend, but I cannot get her to confirm this even after six years. The day finally arrived for our first date. I picked her up, and we went to dinner. She was wearing a nice sundress, which I now know is not normal for her, so she was out to impress, and she did impress! We finished dinner and headed to a local watering hole to meet up with some old co-workers of mine. Before going to the bar we had to stop at her place so she could change. She did not want to wear a dress to the bar, go figure. I remained a gentleman and waited for her downstairs as she went up to change. We headed out and had a few drinks. After we left the bar we returned to her house and sat on her couch and talked. We talked until 1:00 am, at which time I asked her if I could kiss her. She agreed and there were fireworks. I knew then that there was something about Heather.

I was on Cloud 9 as I drove back to Naperville in the wee hours of the morning. I was met at the door by Jinx, my cat. I proceeded to tell him all about this wonderful woman. Hey, I was a single guy living alone; who else was I supposed to tell? The next day I called Heather, and we talked for a couple of hours. We made plans to get together, and as I understand it now she viewed these as tentative plans, but that was not my impression. The next day I was still in a daze. I had finally met a good woman, and not from the Internet. I was genuinely excited to see where it would lead. I returned home from work at lunch and checked my email. There in my Inbox was my Dear John letter from Heather. Apparently, she had been seeing someone else and since "He was there first" she "wanted to see where it would go." I was polite and wished her good luck but inside, I was devastated. I again confided in Jinx and asked him how someone I only went on one date with could have this effect on me? To which he responded by licking his butt.

About a month or so passed and I still had not heard from Heather, I figured she had resumed her life, and I was just a flash in the pan. Then I received the now famous run-on email from her. Here she is emailing a guy in IT (Information Technology) from a computer with a broken spacebar. You would think she would have at least used capitalization to help with the readability, but she didn't. Here is a sample of what she sent.

"HiMike,notsureifyouareint
erestedornotbutIamagainsin
gleandifyouarefreeIwouldlik
etogooutagain,ifyouareinter
estedbutIunderstandifyouare
not.Heather"

Of course I had a stalker girl of my own I was trying to shake so I jumped at the chance. We planned a date for that weekend, but this time it was going to be on my turf. We went to a pool hall in Naperville and then to dinner. After dinner we decided to go bowling. I knew I was in for it when she pulled out her own bowling ball and shoes. We bowled and then returned to my apartment. We continued to talk (and kiss) until about 2:00 a.m. She told me she was going home, and I informed her I was concerned about her being so tired and driving so late, and so I said she could stay at my place and I would sleep on the couch.

She must have been taken aback by my question because when I asked why she said "no," all she could respond with was that she did not have a toothbrush. How many women are concerned with oral hygiene at that moment? Having been raised watching *MacGyver* as a kid I immediately went into problem-solving mode. I said I would go across the street to Jewel and buy her one. Stunned, she agreed, so off I went at 2:00 am to Jewel to buy a toothbrush. Never even thinking I just left a stranger in my apartment. I returned from Jewel and handed her the new toothbrush. I believe this was the "You had me at hello" moment in our relationship. As she got ready for bed, I prepared the couch for myself. She came out of the bathroom and said I did not have to sleep on the couch. I was waiting for her to tell me she was going home (maybe another boyfriend was waiting?). Instead she said I could share the bed with her. I was a perfect gentleman, and in the famous words of one of our presidents, "I did not have inappropriate relations" with Heather.

We continued to date and soon progressed to moving in together, getting engaged, and married. It has been over six years from that second first date, and I am even more in love with her now than I ever have been. Thank you, Sandi, for being the one responsible for me meeting my soul mate!

- Mike Paprstein

It is amazing how God works, and honestly, if my illness was what was necessary to bring two soul mates together, then I was thankful God worked through me to do it! We now have two adorable nephews, Mikey and Ian, and a beautiful niece, Olivia. I like to tease Pickle and Feather (that is our nickname for Heather). It would have been a lot easier had they met on their own instead of putting me through all I went through just so my angel nurse could marry my brother. What a blessing that the nurse who I always felt was my angel is part of our family now!

CHAPTER 23

God, Please Send Us An Angel
(Age 32)

"O Yahweh, you are my Elohim; I will exalt you, I will praise your name; for you have done wonderful things, even counsels of old, in faithfulness and truth." Isaiah 25:1

After all of the surgeries were behind me and my blood counts had been stable for some time, Chris, and I started discussing our options with the doctors of trying for another baby. There were mixed recommendations, but we felt our family was not complete, and we wanted to try one more time. We became pregnant (getting pregnant never seemed to be a problem for me, but holding onto the baby due to my blood-clotting problem proved to be the bigger challenge). We were very excited and things were going well, but then we lost the pregnancy (the fifth one) right around eight weeks. We were both very sad about this. Chris did not want to see me continue to go through the agony of getting my hopes up and then facing such heartbreaking disappointment. He made it clear that we needed to be thankful for the son we did have -- our miracle son Tyler. I agreed, but I still felt in my heart that our family was not complete, and I believed God would grow our family somehow.

I kept having a dream about a little baby girl. It was the same dream over and over again. It was an odd dream as many can be … I was not giving birth but instead was an outsider watching the delivery. There was always the same gentleman with red hair handing me a beautiful baby girl. When I took her in my arms and looked at her angelic face, my heart was filled … our family felt complete. I would then wake up. The dream never changed, it was always the same.

I felt strongly that this last pregnancy was the baby girl I kept dreaming about, so I was crushed when we lost her. We were going to name her Samantha. My dad had come up to visit and was out in our garage. He came in looking almost spooked. I asked him what was wrong. He said, "I had this weird thing just happen. There was a vision of a little girl. She looked at me and said, "Don't be sad … I'm on my way." He looked at me and said, "You are going to have a little girl in your family, trust God. I feel that was one of God's angels sent to you to comfort you and to tell you not to give up hope." It put hope in my Heart again, just like the dream of the Angel healing me had done. I gave my dad a big hug and said, "Thanks, Dad – that is just what I needed to hear right now." As I walked back into the house, I thanked God for sending me what I needed to remind me that He was near and had a plan for us.

I prayed really hard for guidance and strength from God asking whether we should try to get pregnant again or consider looking into adoption. At the time I knew we couldn't afford an adoption. We had many medical bills from the last few years not to mention how difficult it was to adopt a baby. I continued to pray daily, remembering to be patient while believing God would guide us into His perfect will. Tyler continued to pray every day for a baby brother or sister, and he did not understand why God was not sending him one. We had to explain to him that God knows what is best for us even when we think we know better. We have to find it in our hearts to trust Him and be thankful for the blessings we already have in our lives – like each other.

CHAPTER 24

Earth Angels
(Age 34)

"And we know that to them that love Yahweh all things work together for good, even to them that are called according to his purpose." Romans 8:28

My brother was getting married to my nurse Angel Heather. We were all so happy! My mom and step dad, Ron, had just arrived in town. Mom wanted to go visit my Aunt Elsie and surprise her so they took a drive over to her house. Mom got out of the car, walked up to the door and rang the doorbell. She could hear the dog barking but there was no answer. Mom peeked in thru the window to see if she could see anyone. She knocked on the door this time. She thought, *this is unusual, Elsie is always home.* She got back into the car, took her cell out of her purse and called my Aunt Marie to see if she knew where my Aunt Elsie was.

"Hello."

"Hi! It's Pam. How are you doing?"

"Oh good honey, how are you?"

"Well, Ron and I are at Elsie's. We're in town for Mikey's wedding but there is no answer. Do you know where she is?"

166

"Unfortunately she fell on the ice getting out of her van and had to go to the doctor so why don't you come over for a visit?"

"Let me talk with Ron and I'll call you right back."

Mom turned to Ron and said, "Marie wants us to come over and visit. I'm pretty tired though and although I'd love to see her I don't really feel like driving all the way to Merrillville. What do you want to do?" Expecting Ron to say he doesn't want to go either because he was just as tired, he surprised her when he said, "We never go see any of them so why not?" Mom said, "Really? You're not too tired?" He said, "No, I really feel we should go so let's go." They started driving towards Merrillville.

My Aunt answered the door with big hugs as the greeting. My family loves hugs! So they sat, visited and got caught up on things. Aunt Marie showed them pictures of her grandkids. Mom said, "They are adorable." Aunt Marie smiled and said, "Thank you." Her smile lit up the room at how much she loves them. Aunt Marie lived upstairs from Aunt Ocie so she said to Mom, "Why don't you go visit Aunt Ocie as well? It's just right downstairs and I know she would love to see you." So they walked downstairs, sat down for a cup of coffee and started talking about the grandchildren and pulling out pictures. Included in the pictures was a panoramic picture of all of my Aunt Ocie's grandchildren. In the picture there were three children who Mom didn't recognize. Mom said, "Who are these three?"

Aunt Ocie said, "Well, they aren't my actual grandchildren but Rhonda has guardianship of them and

I've adopted them as my own so to speak. I just adore them all." She began to explain that the parents were fighting thru some drug addictions and why Rhonda, her daughter, had guardianship of them. She said the mother didn't really think she could keep the 7 month old because she knew she couldn't take care of herself let alone a baby. My Aunt turned to my mom and said, "She even thinks she might be pregnant again." Ron said, "Sandi and Chris can't have any more children and they truly want another child, maybe they could adopt the 7 month old."

Aunt Ocie smiled and said, "No, they are *my* grandchildren." You could tell how much she loved them. Next thing you know she called Rhonda and told her that Mom and Ron were in town. Rhonda wanted them to come by and visit. Well they hung around Aunt Ocie's waiting for Uncle Pete to come home from work so it was getting too late. They had to get Ty off of the bus for me so they called Rhonda to tell her they'd come by tomorrow instead.

The next day they visited Rhonda and when they walked in, there was a 3 year old girl named Haley. And in the bedroom, in a port-a-crib, is a 7 month old baby girl bald as can be with big blue eyes. Her name was Samantha. She had a runny nose and was lying there staring almost motionless. There were 7 ferrets, 5 cats, and 6 dogs running around in the house.

Mom walked into the bedroom and leaned down to look at her. She couldn't help but pick her up and love on her. Mom walked into the kitchen with her and Samantha just stared at her. Ron and Mom sat talking with Rhonda. Samantha just kept staring at Mom. She wouldn't take her eyes off of her. Mom smiled at her and she reached up to try and grab her glasses. Rhonda started sharing the story of how she became guardian. She said, "The mother doesn't think she wants to keep the 7 month old since she can't care for her." Ron said, "Sandi and Chris want so much to have another child and they have lost many." Rhonda said, "My husband really loves that little girl." Ron said, "Sandi and Chris can give her a life that her mother knows she could never give her, this baby would have everything she needs."

Rhonda said, "Funny because I remember someone telling me if I ever heard of a baby that someone didn't want to let them know but I haven't been able to remember who it was. I've even had dreams about it too but can't remember who it is." Mom said, "That was Sandi at Mike's first wedding. You came to our motel room and she told you then."

Ron asked, "Would the parents be willing to give the baby up for adoption?" Rhonda said, "I don't know but my husband is really close with this baby." They all talk awhile but then Mom and Ron had to go. Mom said, "We have to get Ty off of the bus so we need to get going." Rhonda said, "I have a favor to ask. Since you know so much about computers, can you come back and look at Nick's computer? He can't receive e-mails." Mom said, "Yeah, sure." Rhonda said, "I will talk with my husband and the baby's mother. Please try not to mention it to Sandi. I will work on it and then tell her myself once I know more."

Mom and Ron drove back to my house and well Ron couldn't stand it so he told me about the baby. I said, "What? A baby?" I thought *is this really happening, am I hearing correctly?* I smiled and in my

169

heart I knew there was something very special going on here. I asked, "What's her name?" Mom said, "Samantha." The chills ran through me. That was the name we were going to name our baby girl. I thought *could this be the baby that the little girl-angel told my dad was coming? A baby girl named Samantha to replace the one we lost?* I shook my head to come back to reality after staring off for a minute, lost in thought and in amazement at what seemed to be unfolding. A curious smile crossed my lips and I said, "What does she look like?" Mom was looking thru the sale papers at the time and was in awe that she looked down and saw a baby in the K-Mart ad that looked just like Samantha. She looked at me and said, "Actually, she looks just like this baby." There in the ad dressed in pink footie PJs was this adorable baby girl. Chris came in the room so I shared with him what Mom and Ron had just told me. I said to Chris, "Is it okay with you if I go see the baby?" Ron chimed in and said, "Well, I don't know exactly how we're going to do that, but let me think about it."

Later that night Mom and Ron were talking about how I know computers better than Mom so I was the one that should be helping Nick with his computer not her. Mom decided she would call Rhonda in the morning and ask if it would be okay for me to be the one to look at Nick's computer. I could then also see Samantha. Rhonda said, "Yes, that'd be great."

The next day we got Ty off to school and started heading to Rhonda's. As we walked in the house, Mom went straight to the baby. Samantha grinned at her because she remembered her from the day before. Mom walked in the kitchen. My Heart melted and my eyes filled with tears as I saw her for the first time. I thought what a *precious Angel she is*. I asked, "Can I please hold her?" Mom handed her to me. As I took this precious one into my arms, my Heart filled with Love and hope that this was the baby girl I had been seeing in my dreams. We sat and visited for a while but then I needed to get going on Nick's computer so I began to walk downstairs with the baby in my arms. As I began to walk that way, Nick said "no baby". I looked at Rhonda and asked, "Why can't Samantha come downstairs?" Rhonda said, "Nick smokes and he doesn't want the baby down there." I looked at Nick smiled and said, "That's right Nick, the baby shouldn't be around smoke."

I turned to mom, handed her the baby and then walked downstairs. When we finished with the computer, I walked upstairs and asked Mom if I could hold her again. She smiled and said, "of course" so I took her into my arms. Cody, Samantha's brother, came home from kindergarten and wanted us to watch him ride his motorcycle. We all went outside and stayed outside until the last minute before we had to leave to get Ty off of the bus.

That night, unbeknownst to me, Mom and Ron talked to Rhonda a few times and Ron kept sharing that Chris and I could give Samantha a fresh start on life and that she would have everything she needed. She would have a wonderful life. Rhonda called us and said, "My husband has agreed, but we need to talk with Samantha's mother. I will call you after I do."

Mom and Ron were heading back home to Oklahoma on Thursday. I begged them to stay to see what was going to happen with Samantha. Mom said, "Honey, it's going to take some time but we'll let you

171

know as soon as we hear from Rhonda." Mom and Ron arrived home and Friday night around midnight mom's cell phone started to ring. She got up to answer it and it quit. The house phone then started to ring and then quit. She checked the caller I.D. and it was Rhonda. Mom called her back and Samantha's mother had some questions. She wanted to know what kind of house we lived in, what our occupations were, and what kind of life we could give her daughter. Mom told her, "They live in a $350,000 house. Sandi is an EDI expert and Chris is a Mechanical Engineer. Samantha would want for nothing."

Mom received several calls that weekend. Rhonda said that Samantha's mother was going to talk with her husband about it. And as mom says, "It was history from there!"

On Sunday we received a call from my cousin asking if we wanted to come see the baby. I responded immediately, "YES!" She had talked to the birth mom and, although she was a little hesitant, she was open to meeting us. I wanted to jump up and down but knew not to get my hopes up. I hung up trying to let it all sink in that there was a chance (even if it was small) that God could be sending us a baby. They asked if we could come over that afternoon. Chris and I discussed it and then sat Ty down to explain to him that we were going to visit my cousin, and that we would be meeting a baby that afternoon ... a baby that we MIGHT be able to adopt to be his little sister, and then we explained what adoption meant. It was all happening so fast we still had not fully absorbed it all, so we didn't expect Ty to understand. I felt like I was dreaming.

When we walked into Rhonda's house, Samantha looked so sad though; she just sat in her highchair, not smiling, not holding a bottle, and not doing most things a seven-month-old baby would do. We spent some time with her, holding her and playing with her. When we left, I was sad to leave but I kept trying to shut off my heart fearing I was getting my hopes up just to have them crushed. We got into the car and Ty blurted out, "That is my baby sister!" He would not stop grinning. I explained to him that we couldn't get our hopes up because the birth parents weren't even sure they wanted her adopted by anyone other than my cousin. Ty said, "She is my sister, Mom. God answered my prayer and sent her from heaven like an angel. I feel it!" Hope filled my heart because that is what I always say when God has placed something so strongly within my Heart that I know it to be true even if it seems impossible. I say "I feel it". I thought *wouldn't that be something?* as a big smile spread across my lips. I hoped it would be true because I didn't want him to go through any more disappointments after all that he had already faced due to my health problems and the five miscarriages.

Once we got home and put Ty in bed, Chris and I sat and discussed this little Angel. Chris was concerned that the drugs had most likely had a very negative impact on her, and that she may have health issues which might be difficult to handle along with my health issues. I told him I trust God, and if it ends up that we are meant to have this baby girl regardless of health issues then what a blessing it will be. He remained open to the idea, but I could tell he was guarding his heart quite a bit. I continued to pray that God would guide us and that he would open his heart to this baby girl.

On Wednesday of that week, my cousin called me to see if I wanted to take Samantha for an afternoon, so of course I jumped at the chance. I drove to pick her up; I still had the car seat from when Ty was a baby, so I hooked it up in the car and was off to get her. When I was strapping her into the seat she smiled at me. I called Chris when we were on our way home and told him, "Chris, I feel that she is not going back there again but will be staying with us." He said, "Honey, I know you are very excited but, please don't talk that way. You are just setting yourself up for disappointment." I heard what he was saying, but I refused to believe it because I felt that "tug" on my heart, and I knew as sure as I was sitting there that she was coming home ... *the* home that was meant for her all along.

When I unbuckled Samantha and walked into our house with her in my arms, I cannot even explain how this little seven-month-old baby would know, but she came to life. She was so excited, smiling, bouncing in my arms as if she could not wait to get into the house she had been waiting so patiently to live in. I walked around each room of the house saying things like, "This is our living room and where we will all be spending a lot of time together as a family. This is our kitchen where Mommy cooks food for all of us." I then walked upstairs and, as soon as I turned the corner towards the bedroom that would be hers if we were able to adopt her, she started getting very excited. I walked in the room and said to her, "If God blesses us with you – this is going to be your bedroom, which is right across from your brother's room." She squealed and smiled as if she knew exactly what I had just said. I wished Chris were with me videoing it because the reaction of this little soul was one who seemed to know she was exactly where she was supposed to be. We had a great time playing together all afternoon. I had her sitting up on a blanket in the living room, talking, playing, hugging, and kissing her. In just a few hours of giving her the extra love and attention she deserved, it was amazing to see the change in her.

I heard the garage door and knew it was Chris and Ty. Ty ran in and went straight to the restroom, not even noticing Samantha as he zipped past, but Chris walked in after him and immediately saw Samantha. They just stared at each other – as if the whole world around them stopped for this special bonding moment between a dad and his daughter. She just grinned and would not take her eyes off of him. At that very moment, I saw a bond between those two that assured me, without a doubt, that this was our baby, and she was finally home. That night my cousin called and asked if we wanted to keep her for the night. The next day she called and asked if we wanted to keep her another day, and that kept happening until the following Friday. My cousin, the lawyer, and the birth mother all came to our house to sign papers for guardianship.

Just as God had placed within my Heart, Samantha was at our home to stay. How blessed we are to have this special Angel in our loving care.

~~~~~~~~~~

I sat in awe at what God was doing. Here through what seemed like an unfortunate set of circumstances … a mom and dad fighting a bad drug addiction, leaving their babies in an alley to find their way to my cousin's house that would then allow a precious Angel, Samantha Rose, to come into our lives.

~~~~~~~~~~

As I shared earlier, when Samantha was born her birth parents realized they would not be able to take care of three children. They loved this little baby so much that they wanted Samantha loved and cared for by family. My cousin, Rhonda, was like family to them so they hoped she would adopt Samantha. Rhonda loved Samantha (as well as her brother and sister) but she didn't want to adopt the baby. She was already in her forties and her children were grown not to mention my cousin had a more than full plate.

She is someone who has a heart of gold, but she had enough on her maternal plate to focus on her son and my cousin, Nick. He had been in a horrible accident when he was eighteen; he'd been hit by a semi-truck. He remained in a coma for 99 days and the family was told he would remain a vegetable. They never gave up hope! He eventually woke up from the coma, and he kept fighting and had to relearn things we all take for granted like walking, talking, and even using the restroom. He has suffered some physical affects and as a result many people think he is mentally impaired, but he is not. His mind is completely functional, but due to a limp he has and the fact that he has a condition that prevents him from speaking clearly, he is often mislabeled.

Regardless, the kid still does not give up and certainly does not want anyone feeling sorry for him! Since he cannot speak clearly, he carries a typed page of his story in his back pocket. It allows him to share it with anyone he meets. He requires an expensive surgery to correct this condition but does not have the money to pursue it. I told him not to give up his faith in God and to pray for that surgery. I encouraged him letting him know all things are possible with God.

It's amazing how God works and how He can and will work thru any Heart open to Love. It's why we are to never judge and to trust God's plan in everything. My step dad had gone through some hard times that caused him to pull far away from God, but yet God worked through him to help us with the adoption. If he had not insisted on visiting Mom's family that trip in from Oklahoma, we would have never known about Samantha. He couldn't explain it, but he said he just *knew* they had to go. It's a powerful testimony, and you know, I believe that was an important turning point for him. He knew God had worked through him, and it changed something about him that is hard to explain.

It's amazing how God works through people to do His work, but many do not realize it because they cannot see past the messenger. Instead they are so caught up in expecting God to appear and help them that they dismiss the thought that God is all around them. It reminds me of a joke:

There was a man called Jim who lived near a river. Jim was a very religious man.

One day, the river rose over the banks and flooded the town, and Jim was forced to climb onto his porch roof. While sitting there, a man in a boat comes along and tells Jim to get in the boat with him. Jim says "No, that's okay. God will take care of me." So the man in the boat drives off.

The water rises, so Jim climbs onto the roof of his house. Another boat comes along and the person in that one tells Jim to get in. Jim replies, "No, that's okay. God will take care of me." The person in the boat then leaves. The water rises even more, and Jim climbs onto his chimney.

Then a helicopter comes and lowers a ladder. The woman in the helicopter tells Jim to climb up the ladder and get in. Jim tells her "That's okay." The woman says, "Are you sure?" Jim says, "Yeah, I'm sure God will take care of me."

Finally, the water rises too high and Jim drowns. Jim gets up to heaven and is face-to-face with God. Jim says to God, "You told me you would take care of me! What happened?" God replied, "Well, I sent you two boats and a helicopter. What else did you want?"

- Author Unknown

It is amazing how God tries to reach us, isn't it? I felt blessed by all of those special people whom God worked through to help us. He seemed to send us exactly what and who we needed when we needed it most. One such very special person He sent our way was Teresa, one of my coworkers.

I had no idea how much God would work through Teresa. At a time when Chris and I were really struggling financially with a mortgage, daycare expenses, and all of the medical bills, she called me and said she wanted to send us her bonus checks. I said, "Teresa, we cannot accept that. I just don't feel right about it." She would not take no for an answer and kept insisting God wanted her to do this, and she reassured me that this was how God worked. I cried thanking God for this huge blessing because we did not know how we were going to make our bills and not lose everything. He sent us just what we needed at the exact time we needed it.

God sends us everything we need, but the question is -- Do we ignore His help and blessings because we are expecting God himself to appear? How many times has God tried to help us, but we have looked right past His help or turned it away because our minds have not been open to the avenues He may be using to reach us? Please open your mind and your heart to Him, and you will realize all that He is doing and trying to do in your life. When you do, the results in your life will be really powerful!

Many years later He taught me another very important lesson. God showed me how incredible it feels to bless others. He has given me a heart to give so it's just what I love to do. The feeling you receive when blessing another no amount of money in the world can buy. It just feels good from deep in the soul.

He opened my eyes through something a dear friend, Kathy, said in one of our conversations. She felt in her heart to do something nice for someone but they kept insisting that they just couldn't accept it (as I have also done many times when people have tried to give me things). They didn't feel right taking it. She then said to them, "Don't take my blessing away." The Truth ran through me like a bolt of lightning. I thought, *oh my goodness each time I said no I was taking away their blessing.* It made me want to cry. I was taking away from them the very thing that blesses me so much when I give to others.

God forgive me for robbing people of those blessings and thank you for this very important lesson.

Thank you God for opening my eyes, please help me to receive the blessings You send thru the hearts of others and please continue to provide to me the blessings to bestow upon others. Amen.

"Our True Blessings in Life are hidden treasures held within the Blessings that we bestow upon others."

CHAPTER 25

Blessed with an Angel
(Age 35)

"and above all these things love, which is the bond of perfectness." Colossians 3:14

It would be six months before we would go to court to make the adoption final. During that time we had to be interviewed, have background checks done, and have home visits done to ensure we were fit to be adoptive parents. The timing of Dr. Sweiss coming into my life was amazing. She was able to get my blood disease into remission, which allowed my health to pass the adoption review process. Also, the entire year of surgeries I had endured was necessary, otherwise my shoulders and hips would not have been able to handle carrying around our new baby girl, Samantha. God is amazing, and His perfect timing in this situation was yet another example that despite one of the most challenging times in my life, God had a plan. I never lost faith in Him. I trusted His plan even through all of the pain and suffering I had endured when I faced the AVN and multiple surgeries within a year. Now He was blessing us with this angel baby. God is so good!

During the past six months we had grown to love Samantha so much even though we knew she wasn't legally ours until the adoption was final. The thought of something going wrong with the adoption, thus preventing her from being our daughter, was devastating. We were nervous, and when we talked together as a family we realized we were worried that we could lose her. Those thoughts were overwhelming at times, especially in the weeks leading up to the adoption. During our drive to the courtroom, worry and anxiety were building in all of us. What would our family do if she was taken from us? I started getting knots in my stomach but knew we had to trust God and His plan. I silently prayed, *"God, please be with us as we walk into the courtroom today. Take all of this anxiety and worry and replace it with peace and trust in You."* Amen.

The courtroom was the first time we were meeting the birth dad. As you know, we had already met Samantha's birth mom. When we walked into the courtroom, I was in awe of God, once again. I couldn't believe what I was seeing – there, in front of us, stood the red-haired man from my dream, the one who handed me the angel baby! At that moment, peace radiated my soul. I felt God take each step with me as our family, including Tyler, approached the bench. God reminded me not to worry about anything but to give my worries to Him. He was in control of our lives -- not the courts … *only God*. He would not forsake us if we believed in Him and trusted His plan.

The adoption day turned out to be one of the best days of our lives. The lawyer said that in twenty years of doing adoptions he had never seen an adoption that was as meant to be as this one. Both birth parents showed up in court to sign the papers and make it official. Every single thing that needed to fall into place DID, not to mention that the whole adoption was done for less than $5,000.

Tyler was right! God answered his prayer and sent us our Angel, Samantha. It was as if she descended out of the sky when our hearts needed her most. We had her picture taken in wings so we could include a picture of our little angel in the adoption announcement. Our hearts were filled when she came into our lives. We cannot imagine life without her in it. It feels so right and so perfect, like she was meant to be part of our family from the moment she was conceived. Despite the odds against her of the drugs her birth mom had taken while Samantha was in the womb, she was born without a trace of drugs in her system. She is a thriving, healthy, and beautiful girl who looks like a true angel. Her blonde curls and blue eyes draw people to her. I found that every time I was out with her in the stroller people would stop me to say how beautiful she is.

As soon as Samantha came into our lives in 2003, our family felt complete. I did not have any major health issues for a couple of years. It was a great gift to be able to spend time bonding as a family without worrying about any health issues, which was quite a change from what we were used to, but God knew our family needed that time. We were blessed! God grew a very special bond between Samantha and Chris ... a love that no one else in the world could bring because it was Divine Love between a daughter and her father. Regardless of DNA, Chris was born to be Samantha's daddy and she was born to be his daughter. Many years later I would discover why that bond would be so important for Chris.

"For this child I prayed; and Yahweh has given me my petition which I asked of him." 1 Samuel 1:27

~~~~~~~~~~

Please know that no matter what you face there is a plan and God will send you what you need to get through the challenges you face in this life. And never forget that even if you stop searching for Him, He will find you!

Father John Powell, a Professor at Loyola University in Chicago, writes about a student in his Theology of Faith class named Tommy:

Finding God

Some twelve years ago, I stood watching my university students file into the classroom for our first session in the Theology of Faith. That was the day I first saw Tommy. My eyes and my mind both blinked. He was combing his long flaxen hair, which hung six inches below his shoulders. It was the first time I had ever seen a boy with hair that long. I guess it was just coming into fashion then. I know in my mind that it isn't what's on your head but what's in it that counts; but on that day I was unprepared and my emotions flipped. I immediately filed Tommy under "S" for strange ... Very strange.

Tommy turned out to be the "atheist in residence" in my Theology of Faith course. He constantly objected to, smirked at, or whined about the possibility of an unconditionally loving Father/God. We endured each other in relative peace for one semester, although I admit he was for me, at times, a serious pain in the back pew.

When he came up at the end of the course to turn in his final exam, he asked in a cynical tone, "Do you think I'll ever find God?" I decided instantly on a little shock therapy. "No!" I said very emphatically. "Why not?" he responded. "I thought that was the product you were pushing."

I let him get five steps from the classroom door and then called out, "Tommy! I don't think you'll ever find Him, but I am absolutely certain that He will find you!" He shrugged a little and left my class and my life. I felt slightly disappointed at the thought that he had missed my clever line -- He will find you! At least I thought it was clever.

Later I heard that Tommy had graduated, and I was duly grateful. Then a sad report came. I heard that Tommy had terminal cancer. Before I could search him out, he came to see me. When he walked into my office, his body was very badly wasted and the long hair had all fallen out as a result of chemotherapy. But his eyes were bright and his voice was firm, for the first time, I believe.

"Tommy, I've thought about you so often; I hear you are sick," I blurted out.

"Oh, yes, very sick. I have cancer in both lungs. It's a matter of weeks."

"Can you talk about it, Tom?" I asked.

"Sure, what would you like to know?" he replied.

"What's it like to be only twenty-four and dying?"

185

"Well, it could be worse."

"Like what?"

"Well, like being fifty and having no values or ideals, like being fifty and thinking that booze, seducing women, and making money are the real biggies in life." I began to look through my mental file cabinet under "S" where I had filed Tommy as strange. (It seems as though everybody I try to reject by classification, God sends back into my life to educate me.)

"But what I really came to see you about," Tom said, "is something you said to me on the last day of class." (He remembered!) He continued, "I asked you if you thought I would ever find God, and you said, 'No!' which surprised me. Then you said, 'But He will find you.' I thought about that a lot, even though my search for God was hardly intense at that time. (My clever line -- he thought about that a lot!)

"But when the doctors removed a lump from my groin and told me that it was malignant, that's when I got serious about locating God. And when the malignancy spread into my vital organs, I really began banging bloody fists against the bronze doors of heaven. But God did not come out. In fact, nothing happened. Did you ever try anything for a long time with great effort and with no success? You get psychologically gutted, fed up with trying. And then you quit Well, one day, I woke up, and instead of throwing a few more futile appeals over that high brick wall to a God who may be or may not be there, I just quit. I decided that I didn't really care about God, about an afterlife, or anything like that. I decided to spend what time I had left doing something more profitable. I thought about you and your class, and I remembered something else you had said: 'The essential sadness is to go through life without loving. But it would be almost equally sad to go through life and leave this world without ever telling those you loved that you had loved them.' So, I began with the hardest one, my dad. He was reading the newspaper when I approached him. 'Dad.' 'Yes, what?' he asked without lowering the newspaper.

'Dad, I would like to talk with you.' 'Well, talk.' 'I mean, it's really important.' The newspaper came down three slow inches. 'What is it?' 'Dad, I love you; I just wanted you to know that.'" Tom smiled at me and said it with obvious satisfaction, as though he felt a warm and secret joy flowing inside of him.

"The newspaper fluttered to the floor. Then my father did two things I could never remember him ever doing before. He cried, and he hugged me. We talked all night, even though he had to go to work the next morning. It felt so good to be close to my father, to see his tears, to feel his hug, to hear him say that he loved me. It was easier with my mother and little brother. They cried with me, too, and we hugged each other and started saying real nice things to each other. We shared the things we had been keeping secret for so many years.

"I was only sorry about one thing --- that I had waited so long. Here I was, just beginning to open up to all the people I had actually been close to.

"Then one day I turned around and God was there. He didn't come to me when I pleaded with Him. I guess I was like an animal trainer holding out a hoop saying 'C'mon, jump through. C'mon, I'll give you three days, three weeks.' Apparently God does things in His own way and at His own hour. But the important thing is that He was there. He found me! You were right. He found me, even after I stopped looking for Him."

"Tommy," I practically gasped, "I think you are saying something very important and much more universal than you realize. To me, at least, you are saying that the surest way to find God is not to make Him a private possession, a problem solver, or an instant consolation in time of need, but rather by opening to love. You know, the Apostle John said that. He said: 'God is love, and anyone who lives in love is living with God and God is living in him.' Tom, could I ask you a favor? You know, when I had you in class you were a real pain. But (laughingly) you can make it all up to me now. Would you come into my present Theology of Faith course and tell them what you have just told me? If I told them the same thing it wouldn't be half as effective as if you were to tell it."

"Oooh, I was ready for you, but I don't know if I'm ready for your class."

"Tom, think about it. If and when you are ready, give me a call."

In a few days Tom called and said he was ready for the class, that he wanted to do that for God and for me. So we scheduled a date.

However, he never made it. He had another appointment, far more important than the one with me and my class. Of course, his life was not really ended by his death, only changed. He made the great step from faith into vision. He found a life far more beautiful than the eye of man has ever seen or the ear of man has ever heard or the mind of man has ever imagined.

Before he died, we talked one last time.

"I'm not going to make it to your class," he said.

"I know, Tom."

"Will you tell them for me? Will you ... tell the whole world for me?"

"I will, Tom. I'll tell them. I'll do my best."

So, to all of you who have been kind enough to read this simple story about God's love, thank you for listening. And to you, Tommy, somewhere in the sunlit, verdant hills of heaven -- I told them, Tommy, as best I could.

If this story means anything to you, please pass it on to a friend or two. It is a true story and is not enhanced for publicity purposes.

With thanks,
Rev. John Powell,
Professor, Loyola University[2]

CHAPTER 26

Trust in Him
(Age 37)

"Yahweh also will be a high tower for the oppressed, A high tower in times of trouble; And they that know your name will put their trust in you; For you, Yahweh, have not forsaken them that seek you." Psalm 9:9-10

Although women are told every year at their annual female exam to frequently do breast exams, I shamefully admit that I wasn't one who actually did. Every now and then I would do an exam but more because I bumped into something and it felt a bit tender than for any other reason. One day I had a strong pull on my heart (that wonderful Heart Tug again! :) to do an exam and it wasn't because of an "ouch! I bumped into something" moment; although I have had countless "ouch! I bumped into something" moments. Trust me when I say it certainly was NOT because I have a DD cup or anything. I am a modest size B cup. Regardless, somehow I still managed to get them hit, poked, or prodded in some unexplainable way with a sneaky suspicion that Murphy's Law just may be involved.

I asked Chris to see if he could feel it too but he could not. I did the exam again and thought it was odd I couldn't feel it any longer. I know I felt it! My Heart kept telling me I needed to have a mammogram. It had actually been on my heart for a few months but I hadn't yet called to make the appointment. I tried convincing myself that since he didn't feel a lump and now I'm not feeling a lump that I was sure I was worrying about nothing.

A few weeks passed by, and I kept feeling like I needed to get it checked out. The tug on my Heart was relentless. Although I didn't have a good reason to request a mammogram other than the persistence of my heart, I called and made an appointment with my gynecologist. When I saw her, I explained that sometimes I could feel lumps in my right breast, but then they would go away. "Yes, that is completely normal, especially if it is around your ovulation cycle." the doctor said. I looked at her and said, "I can't explain why, maybe due to my health history, I guess, but I feel like I need to have a mammogram." She could tell by the look on my face that I really felt I needed to get one to check things out. She told me generally they do not recommend mammograms until forty years of age, but she thought it was a good idea due to my history. I was scheduled to have the mammogram a couple of weeks later.

~~~~~~~~~~

The nurse called my name to take me back for my mammogram. She got me settled into a room where I quickly changed into the hospital gown that she had draped over the chair before she left the room. The technician came into the room and explained the tests she was going to be doing. When I say what happened over the next 15 minutes was a bit of an odd experience, well that is an understatement! She opened a bandage package and positioned a sticky circle on each of my nipples. The only time I've seen anything remotely close was when every news channel was covering the story of the 2004 Super Bowl mishap with

Janet Jackson and Justin Timberlake which, by the way, introduced me to the term pasties. Up until that point, I seriously would have thought that it was another name for a deceased person or something. Growing up in the sticks or as my dad says the boondocks did shelter me a bit from things city folk may be privy too. I looked down to get a closer look and thought, "*Is that a BB on there?*" I've heard of arms being referred to as guns but seriously the breasts? Sure enough there was a small metal ball protruding from the white sticky tape adhered to each nipple.

Oh, it gets better. She then asks me to step forward and rest my breast on a clear plastic flat plate. I thought *they're not tired, really. They don't need to rest.* She then says, "This may be a little uncomfortable" as she managed to shape my breast into shapes that not even the top Play-Doh champion could have done. *This girl deserves a metal*, I thought. I watched in awe at how I felt I had just walked into a rerun of Bugs Bunny or some cartoon show where the characters could get stretched into any shape and then instantly snap right back into normal. I did not know where the cartoonists got their inspiration, well until now.

She took quite a few pictures of each breast and told me that the doctor would be calling me in a week to discuss the results. "Thank you," I said to her as she walked out the door and pulled it closed behind her. I got dressed and thought, *This wasn't so bad, a bit odd YES!, but not so bad.* I was a little worried when I had heard what they would have to do to get the pictures. I'll just say I heard it wasn't fun and nothing you would stand in line to do! So as I walked past the reception desk, I was smiling. I had a little jump in my step

193

feeling silently proud that I had survived my first mammogram!

The following week the doctor called me and told me they saw a cyst in my left breast, but it looked completely normal. She recommended a follow-up mammogram in a year due to the immunosuppressive medicines I have to take. Immunosuppressive drugs come along with the risks of developing cancer, especially the one particular medicine I was taking.

My Heart didn't agree, it kept pressing me that something wasn't right and I needed to get a second opinion. I called Dr. Sweiss and explained to her that I'd like to have a follow-up mammogram done soon at the University of Chicago, although I had just had one. She was wonderful as usual and listened to my concerns. She agreed that we should evaluate the cyst they found a little bit further. An appointment was made for me the next month to see a doctor in the Breast Clinic at University of Chicago.

The doctor examined me and sent me down the hall to have the mammogram done. After the test, the technician brought me back to the room so the doctor could review the results with me. The doctor said the left cyst they saw did look normal, but he wanted to have an ultrasound done to ensure everything was okay. The nurse escorted me into the ultrasound room. I had never heard of an ultrasound of the breast. Anyway, I lay back on the examining table while the technician prepared the ultrasound wand with a warm, jelly-like ointment. He then did an ultrasound of the cyst they saw in my left breast. The cyst showed blood flow going to it, which was a bit odd. Typically cysts did not have blood flow going to them like mine showed.

At my request, the breast specialist paged my doctor to discuss the findings with him. He is not only a hematologist but also an oncologist, one who had followed my case for years and is highly respected in his field. I did not want anything (particularly anything that could be related to cancer) done without it being discussed with him first. They decided it would be best to remove the cyst using a procedure called a lumpectomy. A lumpectomy is a common surgery for breast cancer where it removes the lump and the surrounding tissues. "Wow, another surgery?" I said as I shook my head. He said, "Yes, but it is not an invasive surgery so it should be much easier than your others." However, he explained that it was still considered major surgery and that I would be going under anesthesia for the procedure. I was beginning to think God put me on this earth to fund the medical field, particularly the surgeons and the anesthesiologists. *Alright then, let's help another team of doctors earn their paychecks!* I thought. I knew all of the risks involved with surgery, so although he had to share them with me, I had become all too familiar with surgery and the risks that came along with it. Well, I was at least "trying" to listen with a smile.

My surgery was scheduled for November. Somehow the timing of my surgeries or health episodes seemed to fall around the holidays or early spring, particularly March! Due to an acquisition of our company a year prior, my new co-workers were not privy to the health problems I had faced years previous – thank goodness! My health had improved dramatically. It allowed me to go back to work full-time and even travel to the corporate headquarters in Yardley, PA for quarterly visits. I was leading a normal life -- a life of health; a life filled with people at work

195

who knew me for me and not my disease. I had new friends and new close girlfriends in addition to all of the wonderful people God had already blessed me with. I felt like I had been given a fresh start in life.

I got a little overwhelmed when I left the doctor's office because all of my health issues from years ago came flooding back as if they had happened yesterday. I wasn't ready to share this part of my life with my new co-workers, my new friends, or my new boss. I wanted only to have this life that was so normal and so wonderful without losing my identity to my health issues again. Some would love attention like this, but I'd had more than my share of attention over the years, and it was the last thing I wanted.

I knew the chances were high that it could be cancer because of the immunosuppressive medications I had been on. However, I have to say I have no regrets about taking those, no matter what the outcome, because they helped give me my life back. I decided I needed to share what I was going through with those I was closest to at work. After all, I would need a good support system at home and work if I was diagnosed with cancer, right? It was a difficult decision to make. If they knew all of the surgeries and everything I had been through, they would know the last thing I wanted was attention from this, so I was glad they didn't know.

Although I was nervous about it, my next trip into the office, I had made plans to explain to each of my coworkers and good friends what was ahead for me. I prayed that God would be with me, because I knew it would be difficult opening up about some of my health issues, and that because of it, I may lose some friendships. I'd had some friends who couldn't handle it

196

all very well through the years and so they had distanced themselves from my friendship. Some of the new friendships I had gained in my new job were very close to my heart, as if I had known them my whole life, so the thought of any of them distancing themselves from me was difficult to bear. I also did not want them to look at me differently and see me only for my health issues. If I just didn't have to have surgery, I could have kept this entire health thing to myself.

However, along this incredible, spiritual journey, it had become more and more obvious to me that there is a reason for everything. I had a choice; I could try to keep it private, but I also realized how much we need the support of others – especially those we care about. God places people around us and works through them to support and love us during difficult times. Sometimes we may even find God in a stranger offering advice to guide us along our path, but we have to be open to it and what God is doing in our lives at the time. I trusted God in this situation, and the support and love I felt from my new friends and coworkers was incredible. I felt very blessed indeed!

My doctors had been wondering about the possibility of my having cancer for some time due to spots found in my lungs years ago. For years they had been monitoring the spots through regular lung CT scans looking for any type of change. Other patients would have gone through a lung biopsy as soon as the results of the first lung scan came back, but there were too many risks involved with me, especially due to the blood clotting issues. I talked to Dr. Sweiss about the lump found in my breast and my concerns. She assured me all would be fine and explained that the location of this being in my breast couldn't be a more ideal spot.

The lumpectomy went well. The surgeon said it would take about a week for the results.

~~~~~~~~~~~~

The first week everyone was patient while waiting for the results -- well, as patient as we could be, except for Tyler. A few days after I had been home from the hospital, Ty walked in the door from school, and before he said hi, he blurted out, "Mom did the doctor call about your surgery results yet?" He had such worry on his face that it broke my heart. He was eleven years old at the time and understood the word cancer. After he lost his Grandpa Gene to stomach cancer, any time he heard that someone had cancer, he worried tremendously and thought it meant certain death.

I can remember it so clearly. He stood there trying to stand tall and be strong but his eyes started filling up with tears. He was doing everything to stop the tears, but they welled in his eyes. He looked at me and said, "Mom, I can't ever lose you. I need you here. I love Dad and everything, but I need you. You help me through so many things. Please don't leave me, Mom – please." It took every ounce of strength I had not to fall apart because I could feel the pain flowing right from his heart directly into mine. I hugged him tightly and cried, not because of what I was facing, but because of what it was doing to my family. If only each of them could have the same peace I had inside that comes from totally trusting God. It is not easy, but in the moments when you do trust Him completely, there is no other feeling like it in the world. While wiping tears from his face and mine, I said, "Ty, don't worry. We will get through this, honey. We have to trust God and His plans no matter what they may be. Let's focus on the blessings of all of this." He looked at me like I was crazy. I could tell he was thinking, *How can you find something good in a situation that could take you away from me? You're my mother and I need you!* I continued, "This surgery is one that will allow them to safely do a biopsy where other areas they wanted to biopsy weren't safe enough for me. The results of this may give the doctors the answers they need to cure me forever. We don't know what God has ahead but let's trust Him, okay honey?" He looked at me with worry still in his eyes, so I grabbed him for another hug, a long one. I silently prayed, *God please give us the strength to face whatever is ahead. My family struggles deeply, especially since they are still learning how to trust You completely. Please hear my prayer and bring them peace ... bring them You. Amen.* I hugged him for a few moments longer, not wanting to let go.

A couple of weeks passed by and still there were no biopsy results. I was receiving a lot of phone calls and emails from family and friends asking about the results. It meant a lot to me how much people cared. The thing that filled my soul was that in the midst of these challenges and waiting for "the news," those calls provided me another reason to share my belief and trust in God with each one who expressed concern for me. I will not deny, though, that everyone was going through a true test of faith during this waiting period, including me! I prayed for strength and asked God not to let my faith falter. It was difficult to sit and watch what it was doing to those around me who still struggled with their faith so much. I kept praying and trusting that somehow all we were going through would bring them closer to God, just as it had done for me. They just were not there yet. Each day seemed like a week. After the first week when we still had not heard anything, each day started to feel like a month. I kept praying for those around me as well as for myself. We needed to stay strong and not lose sight of Him.

A few weeks after the surgery, my doctor called with the results. He said, "I don't know what it is with you, it seems you are always the rarity, but the results had to be sent out to Mayo Clinic to confirm the diagnosis so it has taken longer than normal. The cyst in your breast showed MALT lymphoma, and this type of lymphoma only manifests in the breast in approximately 1% of patients." Boy if I only played the lotto with these odds I'd be a millionaire five times over! "MALT Lymphoma? What does this mean for me?" I asked him. He said he was not sure, but that he would have to run some additional tests before he could determine what treatments would be best for me.

My dad happened to be there at the time I got this phone call. He has always struggled with my illness and how difficult it was watching me almost lose my life to it a few times. He worried constantly, so I have always tried to encourage him by telling him we have to give our worries to God and trust we are going through things for a reason. Now that I am a mother, I understand how his heart must feel. I can only imagine the agony I would feel watching my oldest child face a life-threatening illness, and how overwhelming would be the thought of possibly losing him. Again, in times like this when we feel so overwhelmed, so worried, so lost -- we CAN do something. We can pray, and we can trust God!

"What is it? What did he say?" my dad asked with great worry on his face -- so much worry that I didn't want to tell him, but I did. I explained that they had found a lymphoma. The look on his face was as if he had just lost his best friend. I said to him, "Dad, it is all going to be fine. Please don't worry! God did not bring me this far to have this happen. Give me a few minutes to research it." I went over to my computer and read multiple articles on MALT lymphoma. I shared with my dad how this particular type looked like the best one to have because it was the most treatable of all of the lymphomas. I saw the worry on his face lift a bit. He said, "But it is still cancer." I looked at him and said, "I know, Dad, but does it really matter? I have God on my side, and He will decide the plan for my life." He just sat there shaking his head because despite his faith, he always seemed to be amazed at exactly how strong mine was and how I trusted God in all of the things that I faced -- things he said he could never imagine having the strength to face himself.

~~~~~~~~~~

Multiple tests were ordered including a PET scan to see if the lymphoma had spread to any other part of my body. A PET scan is a test used to detect cancer. I was injected with a radioactive substance and then asked to wait approximately thirty minutes while it worked its way through my system (basically into my tissues). I was then placed on a cushioned table that slides into a doughnut-shaped machine that would scan my body for cancer. The odds were against me because it is very rare that MALT lymphoma starts in the breast, so there was probably another originating source of the cancer. I think everyone, including the doctors, was expecting the tests to show the lymphoma had spread throughout my body.

I found my faith being tested again as I waited for the results. I knew if the results showed cancer throughout my body that my purpose here on earth may be done. I had made peace with that a few years ago because I believe heaven is a much better place than anything life here on earth can offer. However, what I found myself struggling with was the thought of leaving my children behind without a mother. I prayed as tears streamed down my face, *What about them, God? What about them? Please help me to trust Your plan with everything, because the thought of leaving my children and the pain it would cause them is too much for me to bear at times. Give me strength. I am trusting in You. Amen.* I knew that no matter what the results showed, God would decide when it was my time to depart this earth, not any test result or any doctor. I prayed and believed that despite the odds, God would send me another wonderful blessing that I could share as a testimony to what is possible through Him. It seemed the tension in our house could be cut with a knife. Any time I talked to my parents they were worried about me. My children, particularly Tyler, were having a very difficult time knowing their mom had cancer and could possibly die. I felt peace inside but had my weak moments where I let things build up because I always tried to be strong for everyone around me. I carried this incredible weight on my shoulders seeing what my health issues did to those who cared for me. If I could only take the peace and faith from my heart and put it into theirs, it would be awesome – that was all I wanted for them … peace, the peace that is only possible with God.

My follow-up appointment to discuss the test results went great!! We were very thankful to hear that the scan was within normal ranges. "Praise, God!!" I shouted with joy. The doctor said we had one more test to get through because MALT lymphoma often starts with its source in the gastro-intestinal area. A biopsy was ordered to rule that out. One down, one to go – we can do this! I had the GI biopsies done, and we were blessed again; each of those biopsies showed no sign of MALT lymphoma. It appeared the lymphoma had been contained and no chemotherapy or radiation was necessary at that time. We were very thankful for this gift. God had sent another big blessing our way! It was absolutely amazing!

God continued to prove that when we believe in Him, anything is possible. Tyler was so happy when I told him, he just hugged me for what seemed like forever. "Ty, this is an important life lesson to trust God with all things and never, ever give up hope. He has sent us another blessing; isn't that wonderful?" I said to him as I held him. My heart was filled with so much love and faith. The best way to describe it is in the words of our beautiful four-year-old daughter, Samantha: "My heart feels fluffy, Mommy." Fluffy -- what a great way to describe a perfect heart, one so filled with God that it is completely weightless!

What a blessing that before the lymphoma could take over my body, it presented in such a rare but safe place that it could easily be removed -- a place that also happened to be one of *the* safest biopsies for me due to my complicated health history. It was so safe that my doctors felt the benefits outweighed the risks and allowed the surgery. Had it presented anywhere else, by the time they would have found it, it would have most likely been in advanced stages, but this MALT lymphoma presented in my breast -- yes, which happens in only one percent of patients, but those odds allowed them to safely perform the biopsy and provide a diagnosis that could save my life. This diagnosis gave me the chance to be proactive in fighting a cancer that can turn aggressive very quickly and thus become difficult to treat, which would then reduce the odds of survival. The doctors now know to monitor me for the signs of lymphoma because early treatment in such a condition is critical.

I could have easily focused on the negative instead of trusting God's plan for my life. I knew all things happen for a reason and not to question things like, "Why me out of all of the patients in the world (1%) would have MALT lymphoma in my breast? Why couldn't it just be a cyst like the majority of women have?" I focused on whatever good was going to come out of it all. Whenever I found myself getting weak (even the strongest believers have weak moments), I let God carry me. I kept my faith and knew exactly how blessed I was being in the small percentage of patients where it presented in the breast. God is amazing; I felt yet again like I had hit the lottery!! His continual blessings seemed too good to be true!

Who would have known that little "Miss Positive Mental Attitude" from years ago would have grown that attitude into an even stronger one as a result of the seed God had first planted deep in my heart and that grew roots to ensure it stayed strong and then slowly bloomed throughout this incredible journey into a beautiful flower containing multiple petals ... faith, belief, trust, strength, perseverance, love, compassion, empathy, peace, and happiness, all surrounding the magnificent center which was God. Attitude is so important, and with God we can have a great attitude, can't we? Through God we can have an indescribable peace, our perspective changes forever in a very powerful way. We become the good finders because we look for the good in all situations. A perspective that looks for good is worth its weight in gold because it will find the blessings in every situation, even the darkest of situations.

CHAPTER 27

New Beginnings
(Age 38)

"Blessed be Yahweh Because he has heard the voice of my supplications. Yahweh is my strength and my shield; My heart has trusted in him, and I am helped: Therefore my heart greatly rejoices; And with my song will I praise him." Psalm 28:6-7

It seems throughout the years, March had always presented itself with challenges – particularly health issues for me. March 2007 was no different from any other year. Chris and I found ourselves taking a step back in order to also take a deep breath and say, "Did that all really just happen?" March Madness had its own meaning in our household that is for sure! Every year for some time now it seemed there was something major we faced in March. I am beginning to wonder if it is meant to bring a reminder of "new beginnings" in the spring ensuring our focus is where it is supposed to be in life instead of getting caught up in the rat race we know we can all get pulled into daily.

My health had been very stable, and we were once again in the midst of running in a bunch of different directions with our jobs and with the kids' activities, but we were blessed nonetheless for all of it. I then became ill quite suddenly. It started out as abdominal pain and discomfort, but it quickly turned into full abdominal distention (swelling) with vomiting and a fever. It seemed I had caught a pretty horrible flu virus that had no mercy whatsoever on my intestines. I wasn't able to eat any solid foods for days. First I was not able to hold anything down, then I started to feel a little better a couple of days later when my body would begin craving food but yet making it a known fact that it wanted nothing to do with it! Any solid food caused horrible pain and gassiness. I felt again like I had years ago where I was the "blueberry girl" because I was so bloated. I felt like saying, *would someone just put a pin in me so I can feel better?* We did not know what was going on but suspected the flu was causing my blood disease to kick into full-attack mode, as was usually the case.

As I lay there quite ill, I kept checking for the normal signs of my blood disease activating (i.e. jaundice, shortness of breath), but my color was pale as happens with anyone who has the flu. "Chris, I feel so sick – this flu is absolutely horrible," I said after a couple of days of being in bed. I kept praying every day that I would get a little better and that God would relieve this pain from my stomach – *What a strong flu it is indeed!* I thought. A couple of days later, I tried once again to introduce solid foods but my body wanted no part of it. The good news was that my stomach was half the size it had been a couple of days ago. I had looked about six months pregnant earlier that week.

I tried to muster up some energy to take a bath but couldn't do it without help. "Would you please help me with a bath? I know I am still sick, but I feel gross, and I think a warm bath might help me feel better," I said to Chris when he came upstairs to check on me. God bless him! He has taken such good care of me -- all without ever complaining. He was working all day, and then coming home and taking care of the kids, me, and everything else in the house.

"No problem. Give me a few minutes to clean up after dinner and get the kids settled," he said. Boy did this bring back memories to years ago when Chris had to give me baths, dress me, and take care of my every need because I was so ill. I prayed, *God, please hear my prayer and heal me. I am so thankful for the health You have given me the last few years. The thought of going back to a life of being ill again is more than I can bear at this time. Please hear my prayer. I believe in You and Your healing powers. Amen.*

Sitting on the edge of our whirlpool tub, I knew I had to go to the hospital. I could hardly breathe again, just like years ago. Tears rolled down my face. "God, I don't want to go back to a life of being sick. Please help me, please see me through this and make me well again," I prayed aloud through my tears. I felt my stomach hurting but not from the flu; instead, it was from worry. I knew I had to give all of these worries to God and trust Him, but I was having a weak moment. The thought of going into a five-year spiral of being ill was overwhelming. I saw the look on Chris' face and knew he felt the same way. He handed me the phone so that I could page Dr. Sweiss. She called me within fifteen minutes -- what a great doctor I was blessed with! I explained to her what had been going on the last few days. I was hoping she would say that I should wait one more day to see if my body would fight off the flu, but her voice on the other end made it clear I needed to get to the ER soon, particularly with the type of flu viruses that were circulating that year. Even healthy individuals without rare blood disorders were having difficult times fighting off these new sets of viruses. She said, "With you, we cannot take any chances."

So the flurry of calls and plans began. Our family and friends were wonderful and jumped in to save the day yet again for us. Grandpa Ted came up to watch the kids, Aunt Carrie was on call for anything we needed, not to mention we knew all of the rest of our family and friends would have been there at the drop of a hat if we needed anything else at all. We are incredibly blessed!!! I hugged the kids tightly and told them I loved them and not to worry, but that the flu was making me pretty sick, and I needed to go to the hospital to get better. I saw the worry in Ty's eyes. This was something he was all too familiar with, but fortunately nothing he had faced since he was Samantha's age.

I found myself looking into Samantha's eyes flashing back to the life we faced when Ty was her age (four years old) and remembering the countless trips to the ER with no treatment working, wondering if we were about to start that roller coaster ride yet again. My heart broke as we pulled out of the driveway; I turned and looked at my two precious kids with a forced smile and a wave, assuring them that "Mom was going to be okay."

We got to the ER at University of Chicago, and it was quite busy as usual. They are faced often with major traumas including gunshot wounds, major accidents with "life" flights going in and out constantly. Chris and I were prepared to sit and wait for hours until I could be seen, since patients are evaluated and taken by severity of symptoms. I sat patiently waiting for the triage nurse to evaluate me. I could barely walk at this time and my heart was racing out of my chest. I couldn't help but think *this is what I deserve for not taking the time yet again to get a flu shot. When will I ever learn!*

The nurse called me back, took my vitals, and looked at me with worry and concern. My heart rate was over 120 BPM. A normal heart rate average is from 60 to 85 beats per minute. Mine was double the normal rate! She performed what is called a "bedside" blood count and found that my hemoglobin had dropped to critical levels; it was 4.7 with normal levels being from 12 to 16. My hematocrit was around 15, and that should have been between 34 and 46. If I am calculating correctly, my body was about five units low on blood. The last time my counts were this low I was immediately admitted to ICU and the doctors were giving me six units of blood at the same time.

They rushed me back to the ER and started taking multiple tubes of blood to properly cross-match me for blood transfusions. The challenge was that I am a very hard one to cross-match. My blood type is AB+ (one of the rare ones), and due to the numerous blood transfusions I'd had in years past, my body had built up many antibodies against the blood, and thus it could take at least twenty-four hours to find a match for me. I thought, *"Do we have twenty-four hours?"*

My disease was extremely complicated and sensitive to the slightest change. It appeared my disease was in high-active state, which meant my body was aggressively attacking and killing my red blood cells. That means that any introduction of new blood (once they could finally find a match) could be killed off as quickly as it was given to me. Since my blood counts were already critical, the question was whether we should introduce a blood transfusion. The introduction of blood could cause my body to form a full-force attack on all of the red blood cells, including the new blood and my existing blood. There was no room at all for chance because any more destruction of cells could be fatal.

I sat there praying. Even though I knew God was by my side every step of the way, I was still scared. If I felt this way, I knew Chris had to have been dying inside. I could see the pain and worry in his face. The doctors were scrambling, paging my doctors, and gathering all of the specifics of this complicated case that had just come in the door. I was started on IV steroids immediately, which generally is what controls any kind of crisis for me. It suppresses the immune system in hopes of preventing my body from so aggressively killing off my red blood cells. My heart was telling me this was not the normal crash ... although it had been years (thank goodness) since I had faced anything like this, I know my body all too well, and this was definitely different.

After a few hours in the ER and going through numerous tests, I was admitted to a private room with blood transfusions ready for bedside administration so they could closely monitor me. It appeared all of my blood counts were critical, not just my red cells. The doctor came in and said, "Your blood counts are very concerning. Your white blood cell count is extremely high at 50,000 (normal is 5,000 - 11,000). We are not sure if it is related to your lymphoma diagnosis found in 2005."

Chris turned and looked at me very concerned. "Does this mean the cancer has spread?" I asked.

"We are not sure until we run more tests. Your platelets are only 17,000, and they are supposed to be between 130,000 and 400,000," the doctor explained. We knew since my platelets were low that things were now even more complicated because on top of everything else, the risk of internal bleeding was in the mix. I found myself getting overwhelmed at all of the news. It was yet another roller coaster ride just like years ago. One minute we would be told something that was pretty hard to hear and then, just as we were absorbing that, we would find out another thing. I did my best to hold it together for my husband and knew I had to trust God. It had been years since I had been this sick, and after feeling well for so long I was worried about having my normal life yanked out from under me again.

Please give me strength to endure whatever is ahead, I prayed. The doctors ordered an additional chest/abdomen CT scan. I had to gulp down the contrast liquid hoping I could keep it down for them to capture the image they needed. They were questioning whether I had clots in my organs, despite the blood thinner I had been taking for years (since the major episode I had in 1998). They also wanted to see if the lymphoma had spread and taken over my abdomen ... neither being good news.

They came to take me down for the lung/abdominal scan. Chris saw the worry on my face as I left my room. He didn't see the normal "all is going to be fine" face that I usually had despite challenges of this type. I was wheeled down alone to get my scan. I felt anxiety building up the closer we got to the radiology area of the hospital. It got to be too much, so I closed my eyes and prayed very hard ... *God, I cannot do this alone. I need you with me. I am scared! Hear my prayer and let me know you are here. Amen.*

At that moment the feeling that went through my soul was like no other. A wondrous sense of peace come over me that was so calming it was indescribable; it was as if someone had surrounded me with an embrace. I could almost hear Someone whisper, "I am here and all is going to be fine ... trust me." My worries, fears, and anxieties were gone at that very moment! I had my test and came back to the room smiling ear-to-ear. Chris looked at me and said, "What in the world has gotten into you -- did they give you some good pain medications for the test or something?" I hugged him and said, "All is going to be fine. I am so excited to see what God is doing with all of this now. Something really good is going to come out of it ... another chapter for my book." He smiled but still struggled with that whole concept. He believed in God but did not understand why God kept putting me through all of this. He was still struggling with turning to God for help or strength.

Results of the scan showed large amounts of fluid in my abdomen and a mass on my right ovary. Dr. Sweiss was talking to the top ovarian cancer experts at the University of Chicago. All of the fluid in my abdomen caused a major alert that the lymphoma could be active or, even worse, that I was facing advanced stage ovarian cancer. It was not exactly the news we wanted to hear but after that feeling of peace which had come over me, I knew God was with me and all was going to be fine. Dr. Sweiss called me that night just to

213

check on me because she knew what all of these test results were indicating, but she wanted to know how I was feeling about it. I think she felt my struggles from earlier in the day. "All will be great," I told her, "and no matter what the outcome is, God has a plan here, and I am excited to be part of it. I have to trust Him." She understood because she knows how important faith is in all parts of our lives -- the good and the bad, the ups and the downs, just like the issues I had faced throughout the years.

She is an amazing doctor and, without a doubt, she is guided by God in her practice. She has a presence about her that truly is like an Angel. She has tried unique treatments that some doctors may question, like the Cell Cept for my blood disorder, but those treatments have worked! God knows what is best and will guide those who are open to His guidance. As a result she has saved the lives of many patients, including mine. Imagine the type of treatment all patients could receive if medical doctors would combine spirituality and medicine. I trust God is going to have her do something big in this life, and she is going to help many more patients. She already did something very big in my life when God sent her to be my doctor. God worked through her to heal me, and thus she saved my life just like in my dream.

Dr. Sweiss and I discussed how everyone had been praying for a miracle. It brought tears to her eyes thinking of me, my family, and my children because of what seemed to be obvious signs that things were *not* going to be okay for me. Despite the outlook and medical results, we didn't give up hope or faith that God would guide her yet again in my treatment. We all continued to pray for a miracle believing He would answer our prayers.

The next day, a follow-up ultrasound and examination from the gynecology team showed that there was fluid in my abdomen. Before any type of treatment could be started, they would need to obtain some of the fluid around the ovary, but there were too many risks of me bleeding since my platelets were low. They also suspected I had bled internally due to an ovarian cyst that had burst one week prior. A burst cyst had been filling my abdomen with blood for days while I lay there thinking I had the flu! My doctor started a new treatment of steroids and a combination of other medications I had taken before. My counts started to come up every day without any transfusions being required. I was released from the hospital after my blood counts reached normal levels and remained stabilized there for a few days, and I was also scheduled for a follow-up visit with my doctor in a month to check on the ovary and the abdominal fluid levels.

I sat there amazed at how quickly things had turned around for the better. "My blood counts came up in a few days. How in the world was that possible?" Typically it would take months to turn my blood counts around, but through faith and the excellent treatment by a doctor who is not only brilliant but believes in God, miracles seemed to be happening -- miracles that may seem small to the world but were huge to us. My blood counts did not usually turn around so quickly like this, not ever – God is amazing! I realized then just how critical a combination of medicine and spirituality is to the human needs in this world, and I pray that God will work through Dr. Sweiss to lead the way for others in the medical profession.

I trusted that the ovarian cancer would work out somehow, and I knew to stay focused on the blessings that were in front of us at the moment.

"... With men this is impossible; but with Yahweh all things are possible." Matthew 19:26

CHAPTER 28

Crossroads
(Age 38)

"Blessed is the man that endures temptation;
for when he has been approved, he shall receive
the crown of life which Yahweh promised to
them that love him." Jacob (aka James) 1:12

Four days after returning home from the hospital with the internal bleeding from the ovarian cyst, I found myself suddenly overcome with severe abdominal pain and a high fever. I was up all night and by morning called my doctor. She was concerned that I had internal bleeding again and wanted me to go to the closest emergency room. I wanted to cry, but I prayed instead, trusting God to heal me and thanking Him for the blessings just a few short days ago. Instead of going to the University of Chicago, Chris loaded me in the car and we headed to a local ER in hopes of being seen there sooner than I would be seen in a major trauma ER unit in the city.

Unfortunately, the week of March 19th obviously was one of complete madness and chaos. The ER rooms and hospitals were full around the city and suburbs. I found myself waiting for three hours in the waiting room. I lay on the couch in severe pain hoping to be seen soon. When I was finally called back I explained my complicated medical history and all that had transpired the week before. I was put in a bed in the hallway of the ER and pretty much left there. I was in a lot of pain and feeling very sick. When the doctor said they wanted to do an abdominal CT scan and asked me to drink the contrast liquid, the thought turned my stomach. Once again, I could barely get one cup down. My stomach would have no part of it no matter how hard I tried. It was at least the fourth time I was facing a situation of not being able to drink the CT liquid contrast.

The doctors decided to do an ultrasound of the abdomen and ovaries as well. Again, it showed a lot of fluid, just like the week before. The doctors realized a local hospital was not the place for a complicated patient such as me so they put in a request to transfer me downtown to the University of Chicago.

We sat in the ER for twelve hours before they transferred me by ambulance to the U of C ER. It was a grueling ride, with every bump sending stabbing pains through my abdomen despite the IV morphine drip they had started in an effort to ease my pain. It brought back memories from years ago when I felt like the muscles were being ripped from my bones that time when I was loaded in an ambulance in excruciating pain to be transferred to the University of Chicago. I found out later I was the last patient accepted that day into the U of C ER. They had gone into "hold" status on account of the overabundance of accidents, illnesses, gunshot wounds, etc. that had flooded the ER and hospital rooms that week. The first blessing in this second round of my March 2007 journey, I was able to get into the hospital where I needed to be. Looking back today, I cannot imagine what would have happened to me if they had turned me away.

The doctors immediately started pulling blood work and determining what tests they wanted to do. They kept me on IV morphine for the pain. I had to go through repeat ultrasounds and abdominal CT scans. My white blood count was dangerously high as well as my liver enzymes were off the charts (bilirubin of 11.7). I was screaming yellow. It looked as if Samantha had taken a yellow marker and colored every part of me, including the whites of my eyes. It was unbelievable! All of that bile in my system made me feel even more sick, so they were giving me anti-nausea medicine along with the morphine. I lay there just wanting all of this to be over. My heart was breaking as I watched Chris trying to desperately grab a few minutes of sleep in the chair next to my bed. We had been in the ER for two days waiting for a hospital bed to become available. Once again, God gave me the strength to somehow endure these things, but to see the pain it causes those who care about me is difficult to handle.

The doctors were not saying a whole lot but things obviously turned to a very serious point because they said they were waiting for an available bed in ICU for me. I thought, *ICU?* They then brought in a team of ICU doctors to be with me in the ER until they could get me transferred. I was pretty out of it with the morphine, so I'm not really sure what exactly was going on. I knew they said I had an infection in my abdomen so they started IV antibiotics. They also started high dose steroids to help with any blood disease activity that might be happening (based on the amount of jaundice it seemed the disease was in a very hyper state again). At midnight I finally was transferred to an ICU room where the nurses and ICU team of doctors were absolutely phenomenal. They let Chris stay in the room with me but again, no bed or anything comfortable for him to sleep on -- just a chair with a stool that he could try to spread out on. That was not easy for a 6' 3" man! I felt so bad for him, but I knew he did not want to leave, and I didn't want him to either.

I was constantly monitored with blood counts, heart monitors, and multiple medications being changed through the IV bag – there was constant activity, it seemed. I had multiple teams of doctors watching me from many departments: ICU, Hematology/Oncology, Gynecology, Surgery, and Rheumatology. Based on the ultrasounds/abdominal CT scans that showed a lot of fluid, a tumor in my ovary and the ovarian cancer marker (CA125, I think) being elevated, all signs were pointing to advanced stage ovarian cancer. Apparently the follow-up was indicating very strongly that this was ovarian cancer, so the doctors discussed that with us. I thought Chris was going to cry. It seemed after all of these years he was at his end. I prayed, *Please God, don't put him through this anymore.*

The doctors decided it was important to go into the abdomen and extract some of the fluid in order to obtain the answers they required for proper treatment. I continued to receive a lot of pain medicine, high dose steroids and a combination of antibiotics through the IV, but my blood counts were not improving. My bones began to ache worse than you could ever imagine; I felt as if I had no strength left in my muscles at all. I finally insisted that Chris go home that night so that he could get some rest. He looked exhausted, both mentally and physically. I was afraid to send him home because I felt very ill. I didn't know what could happen in the middle of the night, but I wanted him to rest. If something happened to me, I wanted him to be there with the kids.

My heart ached for them so much it was almost unbearable.

After my 2 am blood draw, I found myself just lying in bed crying. I was crying not only from the pain and being sick, but also my heart was breaking from being away from my kids. Even beyond that, however, I felt overwhelmed with that feeling again of *this is it ... I'm not sure I have the strength to go on this time.* Just as you see in the movies, I saw my life begin to flash before my eyes. I could see all of the mistakes I had made, mistakes that no one but God knew. I sobbed deeper than I have ever sobbed in my life. I began to beg Him for forgiveness repenting of all I had done wrong. No one else knew but God knew, He always knows. *Father, please forgive me of all my sins ... wash me clean as snow. I am so sorry for what I've done, will You forgive and heal me?* Then it was as if the movie switched to another scene. The thought of all that I would leave behind, including two young children who would be left motherless, ached to my soul. So I made a vow to myself, *I cannot give up.*

Despite my strong faith, there aren't many Bible verses that I could recite off the top of my head at the time. However, I had found lately that I would turn to the Bible more and more for answers. We all know how prayers combined with a complete belief truly can produce miracles. I had asked Chris to bring my Bible the day before not knowing just how desperately I would need it that night. As I lay there crying, wanting so much to be spared from the horrible ache in my bones, I prayed for God to show me something in the Bible that would give me the strength I needed. Out of over 2,000 pages in my Bible I opened right to Psalm 6, which reads:

221

*" ... Have mercy upon me, O Yahweh; for I am
withered away: O Yahweh, heal me; for my
bones are troubled. My soul also is severely
troubled: And you, O Yahweh, how long?
Return, O Yahweh, deliver my soul: Save me
for your lovingkindness sake. For in death
there is no remembrance of you: In Sheol who
shall give you thanks? I am weary with my
groaning; Every night I make my bed to swim;
I water my couch with my tears. My eye wastes
away because of all my adversaries. Depart
from me, all you workers of iniquity; For
Yahweh has heard the voice of my weeping."*
Psalm 6:2-9

Again, being overcome with that feeling of
peace that is hard to describe, I started to drift off to
sleep. I woke up to a beeping sound that seemed to be
coming from over my head. I pushed my nurse button
so the nurse could come in and check my IV pumps
because that is what the beeping sounded like, but
everything was fine. They were not beeping. She
searched my room for some time and even brought in
another nurse to look. They could find nothing. They
called maintenance. I sat there in bed and clearly heard
God say, *pay attention I'm sending something big!*

Awhile later, the maintenance guy showed up
and looked around the room. He saw an IV pump that
was sitting behind the head of my bed that was beeping,
but it was NOT plugged in. The nurse looked puzzled
because that was an IV pump that had a dead battery,
but yet it had been going off constantly for quite a
while. I smiled and drifted off to sleep as I thought,
*God, I hear you, and I am paying attention. I promise I
will share the testimony of what you are doing.*

I was awakened for another blood draw at 6 am.
An ultrasound was scheduled for early morning so a

222

sample of the fluid could be obtained and a plan to fight the cancer could be put into place. Time was of the essence regarding treatment. Just as the blood draw was completed it seemed there was a knock on my door from the ultrasound technician. He wheeled in the ultrasound machine, which they would use to properly locate the fluid that would be taken out by needle aspiration. The ultrasound technician was obviously irritated because they ordered this STAT and thus had pulled him out of his normal routine to deal with this. He probed (not so gently) all over my abdomen and did so multiple times -- each time with more of an aggravated look on his face. He walked out of my room and said to the doctors in a very irritated tone, "I am so glad you rushed me up here for THIS; there is no fluid in her abdomen." The doctors came into the room to confirm what he was saying because it could not be possible. They did not believe what they were seeing. All of the fluid within my abdomen and the tumor on my ovary were gone! Yes G-O-N-E as in disappeared! The doctors knew there had to be fluid around the ovary still because fluid from cancer does not disappear without being removed or treated.

They transferred me to the gynecology department to have the same technician that had done the ultrasound previously perform it again. The technician could not believe her eyes. The picture had completely changed. I smiled at her and said, "God sent me a miracle." She smiled and nodded, "It sure looks that way. I can't believe what I am seeing." The doctors shared with us that they could not explain it, but there was no longer fluid around the ovary and, as far as that goes, no tumor in the ovary either. They kept talking, checking, and re-checking the ovary with the ultrasound as if they could not believe what was right in front of them. Their training certainly didn't explain anything like this. The ultrasound image from the previous week, and also a couple days prior, had completely changed -- so much in fact that they ordered another ultrasound follow-up for a few weeks later to confirm the medical findings of the tumor and fluid being gone.

The doctors explained that I had a few infections at the same time -- one within my abdomen, ovary, and kidneys. They also told me that my bone marrow had shut down. As a result, my body could not produce the cells needed to fight the infection. It also could not replenish the blood cells which the blood disease was killing off. Now the ICU made complete sense, and I understood why my bones ached so much! I was fighting for my life. That day my blood counts started to return to normal. I was released from the hospital a couple of days later. I couldn't believe that within a couple of days I had gone from facing death in ICU to walking out of the hospital.

A month later, the follow-up ultrasound confirmed that the obvious signs of advanced stage ovarian cancer had completely resolved without any medical treatment. God had sent me another miracle. I was in awe.

Chapter 29

Blessings Too Good
(Age 39)

"and I will make of you a great nation, and I will bless you, and make your name great; and you will be a blessing: and I will bless them that bless you, and him that curses you will I curse: and in you shall all the families of the earth be blessed." Genesis 12: 2-3

When I was facing the lymphoma diagnosis in 2005, Tyler said to me with tears in his eyes, "Mom, God could not possibly send you another miracle. He has used up too many on you already. How will you pull through this one too?" It was another opportunity for me to remind him that with God all things are possible ... there are no limits when it comes to God's undying love for us.

The blessings that we receive seem too good to be true because a whole new world opens up for us. We gain a whole new perspective! We begin to see things differently than we did before. When we trust God with every aspect of our life, we do our best to live in His way. His way challenges us to be good people – the people God made each of us to be.

It is easier to be angry than it is to fill our hearts with love; it is easier to judge than to be supportive in

225

situations we may not understand; it is easier to be hateful than empathetic or compassionate. However, if we can rise above all of that and meet the challenge of being more like Yahushua, we find our decisions and actions fill our hearts with peace and happiness instead of bitterness, which poisons us. Soon our lives begin to fall into place, and challenges that once seemed overwhelming are manageable because we have a renewed strength that is hard to describe.

"And he answered and said to them, To you it is given to know the mysteries of the kingdom of heaven, but to them it is not given. For whoever has, to him shall be given, and he shall have abundance: but whoever has not, from him shall be taken away even that which he has. Therefore I speak to them in parables; because seeing they see not, and hearing they hear not, neither do they understand. And to them is fulfilled the prophecy of Isaiah, which says,

By hearing you shall hear, and shall in no wise understand; And seeing you shall see, and shall in no wise perceive: For this people's heart has grown fat, And their ears are dull of hearing, And their eyes they have closed; Lest they should perceive with their eyes, And hear with their ears, And understand with their heart, And should turn again. And I should heal them."

Matthew 13:11-17

An abundant life is waiting for each of you … all you have to do is open your mind and allow your eyes to see it and perceive it and your ears to hear it and understand it. Yahweh is patiently waiting for you to know the true teachings of His son Yahushua HaMashiach.

When we help others, whether it is a simple act of kindness, a charity donation, volunteering time, or sharing personal experiences to offer support and guidance, God is working through us. God does not physically stand before us and give food to the poor. Instead He tugs on our hearts, guiding us to take the food to the poor. Each one of us has that tug, it is up to us whether we ignore or listen to it. Are you listening? If not, start listening, and the blessings you will receive will seem too good to be true.

~~~~~~~~~~~

I was oblivious to how God works through so many different avenues to reach us. Once I started opening my eyes, my ears, my mind, and my heart to Him, the things that seemed impossible were suddenly possible. I am still in awe at the blessings that have unfolded in my life; blessings which are truly too good to be true and, yes, that includes every challenge!

I have prayed for some time asking God to help me figure out my purpose in life. I think we all wonder that, don't we? I knew my heart seemed a little different than most, especially through these challenges. Many looked at me as if I was crazy when I would say I felt blessed with each challenge that God sent my way. It was because I was excited to see what He was going to do next, what testimony would be revealed proving that God does exist and what He can do in our lives when we believe and trust in Him. The neat part was that by being this way even before realizing the importance of each of these true testimonies, my experiences were helping those close to me find their way to Him, in a way that wasn't preaching or "Bible thumping," as some negatively refer to it, but instead through experiencing it with me as it unfolded along my spiritual path.

I had countless people tell me how important it was to share my true-life experiences with the world, because what better way to prove that God exists? I continued to pray about it. Prior to my surgery in November, my husband and I decided to get baptized again. We were both baptized as babies, but there was real power in making a decision as an adult to prove to the world our belief in Yahweh thru accepting His son Yahushua into our hearts through baptism. I get chills just thinking about how powerful that baptism was to me. I continued to pray that God would help me find my way to my true purpose here on earth.

Shortly before the surgery I had another incredible dream/vision. God was talking to me again just as He had years ago when He worked through Ken to get me back on my spiritual path. God was telling me, *you are special, and you do have a purpose here.* I sat there looking at Him in awe yet also feeling puzzled knowing that I believe each of us has a purpose here, but I wasn't sure what my purpose was exactly. He then reached out His hands towards me, and in His hands was this magnificent, beautiful, warm, indescribable ball of light. It was so real. I sat there in awe, not feeling worthy of His presence. He reached down, and as He was placing the light into my heart, He said to me, "You are my special child. Now it is time for you to go and do your work for me." I woke up with chills, looking around the room to see if He was still there. It was so real and powerful being in His presence -- so much that I felt weak in my knees and couldn't get up for a while. I just sat and prayed and cried. I did not feel worthy of this. I thought *who am I to have a light put inside of me?* It took me a couple of weeks to actually open up about this vision to anyone.

I then had my surgery, and it was during my recovery when Tyler nudged me to get my book finished. I still felt unworthy of that dream, and then while I was praying for guidance to find a Bible verse for one of my new chapters I came across this verse:

> *"For I know nothing against myself; yet am I not justified by this: but he that judges me is Yahushua. Therefore judge nothing before the time, until Yahushua comes, who will bring to light the hidden things of darkness, and make manifest the counsels of the hearts; and then shall each man have his praise from Yahweh."*
> *2 Corinthians 4:6*

I realized then what God was trying to tell me. All I had been through and all of the experiences, including finding a non-denominational church, provided me the knowledge I needed to find and understand Yahushua's teachings. I now have the "Light of the knowledge" of Yahweh filling my heart. I still have much to learn but feel He has prepared me for the next step in my journey. It is time to share His Word and my experiences with anyone who will listen!

I pray every day that God will open up the avenues and allow me to share these incredible testimonies through whatever channels will help others. I do not know the specifics of what God has planned for me, but I know He has a plan. I trust completely in His plan, and I am excited to be part of it! I pray that you have found inspiration in reading my story and that God blesses you along your journey of faith.

One Single Choice

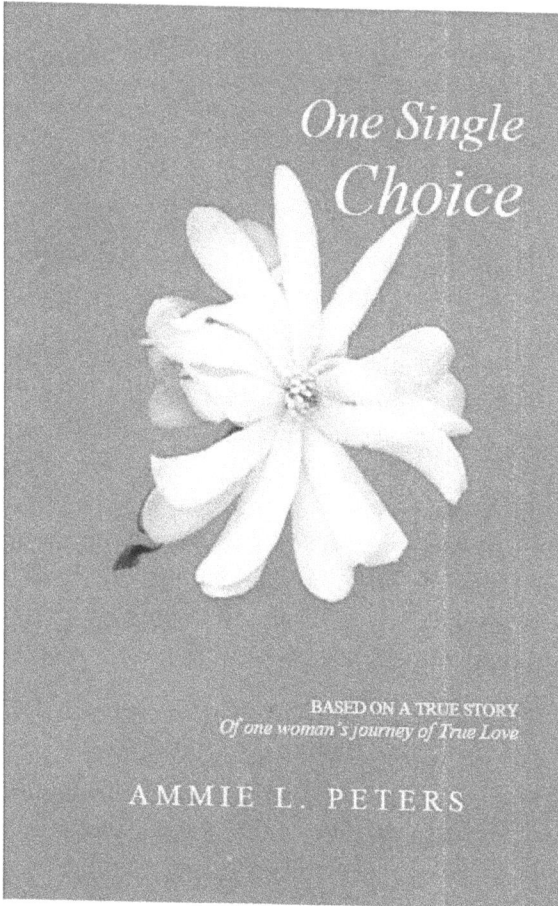

Based on a true story, a young mother of two faced more than most people do in a lifetime. She received miracle after miracle thru the many years of health struggles. She was given her life back and now steps out into the world free of the chains of debilitating illness. She is so thankful for the amazing gift to live again but does not see what is lurking right around the corner. She was young and naïve. She has faith strong enough to move mountains but had so much to learn. She was ready to take on the world but would soon learn how one single choice can take away the life you know in the blink of an eye.

26 Things Life Taught Me

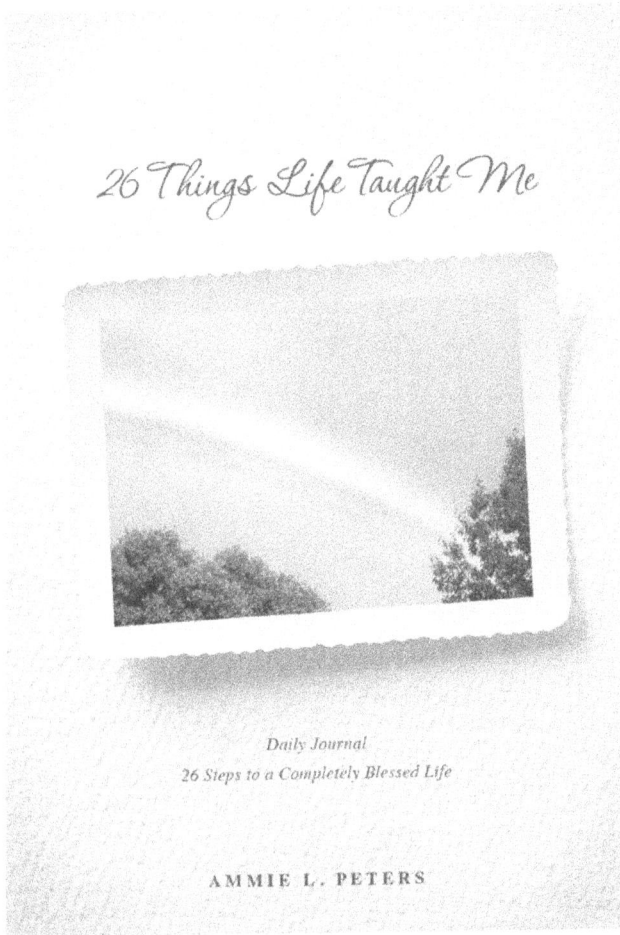

26 Things Life Taught Me

Daily Journal
26 Steps to a Completely Blessed Life

AMMIE L. PETERS

26 Things Life Taught Me is a daily journal walking you through the steps to bring a completely Blessed Life. There are 26 key things at the core of each and every person that needs to be reignited. Once reignited, that fire will burn away anything that has been keeping you from a fully Blessed Life here on earth. This journal will walk you through an amazing journey that will forever change your life. Follow these steps to transform your heart and obtain the Life you have always longed to have but never thought was possible.

Message of the Day

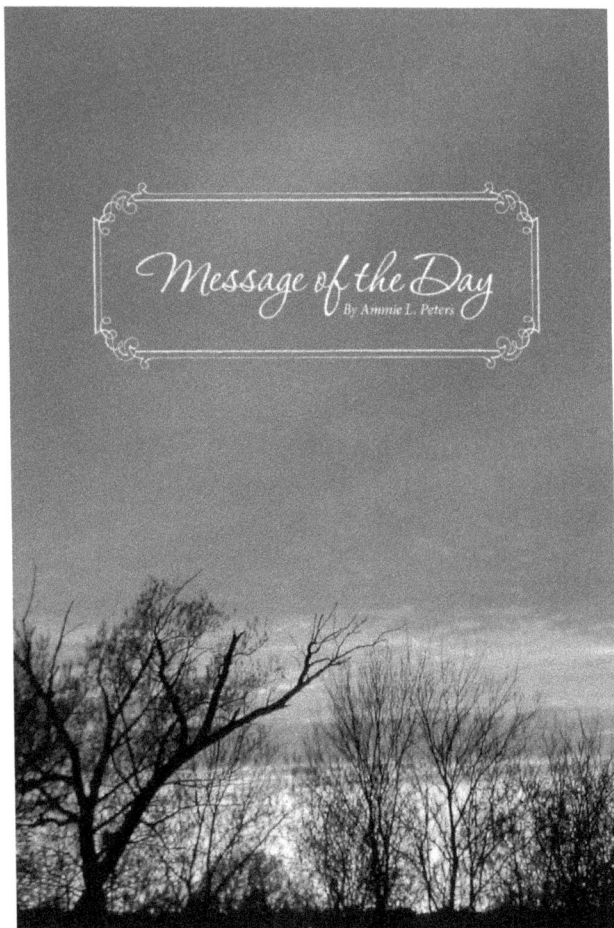

Since the time of Ammie's miracles, messages began to pour into her heart to share with others ... Messages of hope, inspiration and encouragement. She began sharing these messages with the people on her email list. Soon, she began receiving requests to see them in book format. She has now compiled her first book of some of these messages in hopes of encouraging and inspiring people around the world. Her life continues to be a living example of the impossible becoming possible. Her writings inspire true hope and faith within the hearts of her readers no matter where they are on their spiritual walk.

References

[1]American Red Cross. *Give Blood – The Gift of Life.* Retrieved December 30, 2007 from http://www.redcrossblood.org/ 1-800-GIVE-LIFE

[2]*Finding God.* ICBS, Inc. (1998-2008). Retrieved February 27, 2008 from http://www.1stholistic.com/prayer/A2007/spirituality-finding-god.htm

Assemblies of Yahweh (1981-2008). *The Sacred Scriptures Bethel Edition.*

Thank you for helping to bring love to the heart of another. A portion of each book sold is donated to In the Spirit of Love Foundation. We believe that when we desire to give, we have learned how to live. To encourage you to keep the love going, each purchase includes your very own Live it! Card. To receive your card, please email alpeters@blessings2good.com. Ensure you include your name, address, order #, and place of purchase. Once received, register your card online at www.inthespiritoflove.org then do a random act of kindness/love and pass the card to the recipient encouraging them to do the same. Revisit the website. Enter what love you "lived". Periodically check back to track where the card has traveled and what love has followed. Ensure to request your card today so you can Live it!

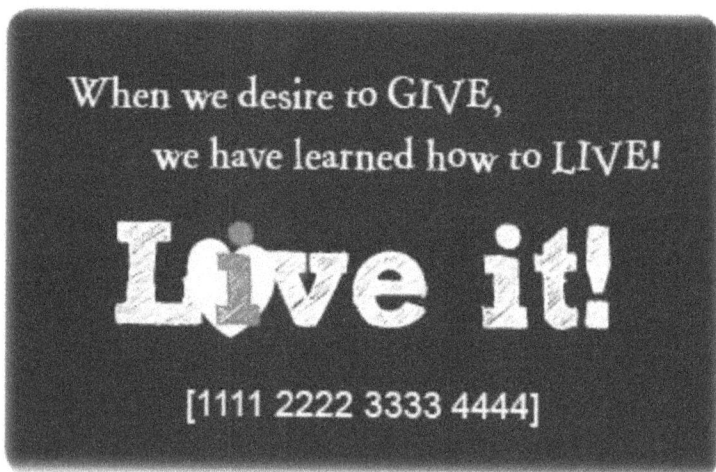

When we desire to GIVE,
we have learned how to LIVE!

Live it!

[1111 2222 3333 4444]

Thank you for being a very important part of bringing much needed love to the world.

Many Blessings to you!

www.ingramcontent.com/pod-product-compliance
Lightning Source LLC
Chambersburg PA
CBHW072342090426
42741CB00012B/2884